HISTORY OF THE IMPOSSIBLE:
Earth Before the Pyramids.

Complete history of the past from 65,000,000 BC to 2,000 BC

By

Igor Kryan, MS

Copyright 2009.

All chapters of the book where written between January 2006 and July 2009

Printed in the United States of America

"Can you belive in the impossible? No? Then, read and find what great wonders were hidden from us: some by layers of earth and time and some by incompetent archeologists. Can you belive in the impossible? Yes? Then, read and this book will forever change your mind about humanity past and possibly about our future." Igor Kryan

Unexplained ancient South American artifact.

"The investigation of scientific progress has found a rule for how such a process develops: at first the data that doesn't fit is ignored, when it gets a bit more it is suppressed by disqualifying its sources, and when finally the amount of data gets too much or some decisive fact is found, the overall community changes its opinion in the sense in that they say that they always silently supported the new view, but it was the colleagues who held them back. This process is so widespread, that there is has gotten its own name: paradigm shift." Frank Joseph.

Contents:

Ancient metal alloy arrow shaped pendant.

Prologue: Shiny Arrow

In year 2000 I was studying Anthropology at CCSF. It was summer semester and professor from UC Berkley took a part time job teaching students in San Francisco. The subject of interest was early California Indians and their environment. I don't remember why but he invited me and one other student to visit UC Museum of Paleontology at UC Berkeley. We gladly agreed and after seeing interesting but predictable display of Indian exhibition at the museum main floor - he took us underground to the museum storage and research facilities.

Professor showed us some very interesting items also belonging to early Indians: such as huge number of glass arrows and spear heads. According to the conventional theory Indians were making those sharp items from volcanic glass to hunt birds and small animals in California swamps. Some of the arrow heads were looking like they were not cut directly from volcanic glass but just molded and sharpened. Of course, early Indians did not have technology to mold glass and that's what researchers at Berkley were studying at that time.

The museum's underground also had plenty of items which were never introduced to the general public display because scientists could not make sense of these artifices. Scientists say such items either misdated - Carbon isotope analysis shows much earlier time then needed or professors simply could not make sense of some artifacts - simply not sure what was the item purpose. Among such strange items there was a shiny object that also resembles arrowhead but it was attached to the rope and, most probably, was worn as an object of great significance by tribal chief or shaman. The grave of "Important Indian" was excavated during early California gold rush era period in late 1840s by gold diggers and then sold with other items from the same grave to the museum and finally ended up at UC Berkley. Since it did not look like a traditional Indian jewelry, for the long time it was considered to be manufactured from some silver alloy in 17th or 18th century in Eastern US and then somehow it ended up as Native American shaman charm who was buried with this strange arrow like pendant. However, since this artifact was so unusual in 1990s somebody decided to run complete lab tests. Lab results left a couple of professors astonished - they found out that it was made from aluminum copper alloy plated by platinum. They, of course, immediately suspected a forgery because aluminum in its pure from was first produced in Europe 10 years after the pendant-arrow was found. Additional tests and investigation results just add up to the shock: first, no known major factory was ever producing aluminum copper alloy and plating it by platinum; second, they found about 100 years old exact description and photo of this item among other excavated items; third, it came from reliable source - other museum; fourth, C-14 carbon dating analysis showed following results - rope is barely couple hundred years old and they could not test charm directly because C-14 radiocarbon dating was not designed to test metal but they scanned the pendant and found a tiny peace of wood like substance included or melted inside the charm - its age was determined to be over 15,000 years old. Needless to say, that to plate something with platinum you need to have an eclectic current. Metal arrow was quickly hidden into a storage from the main exhibition, then forgotten and mystery remains.

I do not mention professor's name because he was not supposed to bring non-paleontology major students from different colleges at UC Berkeley research facilities but maybe he somehow suspected that almost 10 years after I will find the answers to the questions the mainstream science could not answer.

Ancient sculpture of flying creature found in Mexico.

Chapter 1: Strange Similarities.

Earth was a nomadic place of sparsely populated wild tribes of hunters and gatherers for hundreds of thousands years. Then something strange happened: within a thousand years span (about 3000 BC - 2000 BC) in separated parts of the world over half a dozen of mighty and well organized civilizations appeared almost suddenly: Egyptians in Africa, Minoans in Europe, Sumerians (Babylonians) and Akkads (Assyrians) in Middle East, Indus and Chinese in Asia, Mayas in America. Never seen before writing, laws, strict hierarchy, metalwork, military, the practice of irrigation agriculture, the existence of cities, of monumental art and architecture took its clear well recognizable today shapes and forms. The biggest wonder since the appearance of life on earth has happened: Bronze age substituted Stone age that lasted over 5 millions years and human civilizations as we know them today were born.

Mentioned ancient civilization share these striking similarities as well:
1. Great flood story.
2. Priests and temples, the idea of worshipping deities, and blood sacrifices. Similar religious polytheistic beliefs.
3. Sky Wheels: The structures discovered at Nabta (ancient Egypt) are similar in form and possibly function to structures such as Stonehenge in southern England and the Bighorn Medicine Wheel in Montana.
4. Calendar Calculators: The Egyptians, Mayans, and Chinese all came up with ways of marking time; ancient Mexicans and Egyptians both developed a 365 day calendar.
5. Both Egyptians and ancient Mexicans worshipped feathered-serpent deities.
6. Ancient Olmecs of Mexico have much sculpture and artwork in common with ancient kingdoms of West Africa.
7. Similar stone working and stone moving technologies.
8. Knowledge of the earth being a sphere in ancient times was possessed by all or almost all civilizations. Knowledge of the geography of the entire earth in ancient times by many ancient civilizations.
9. Similar ancient pyramids are found everywhere: Africa, South and Central America, Eastern and Central Europe and Asia.
10. Relations between ancient alphabets. Many symbols from different continents look suspiciously similar.

This list is clearly drawing the conclusion from it: in ancient times there was a civilization that preceded all the civilizations on all of these sites. The only problem is that known history and archaeology have no place for such a civilization. According to them (depending whom you ask) the first advanced civilization is the Egyptians or Sumerians, which is dated back to three thousand years BC. The reason because no preceding civilization is recognized is that no recognized remains of a preceding civilization have been found. Or weren't they?

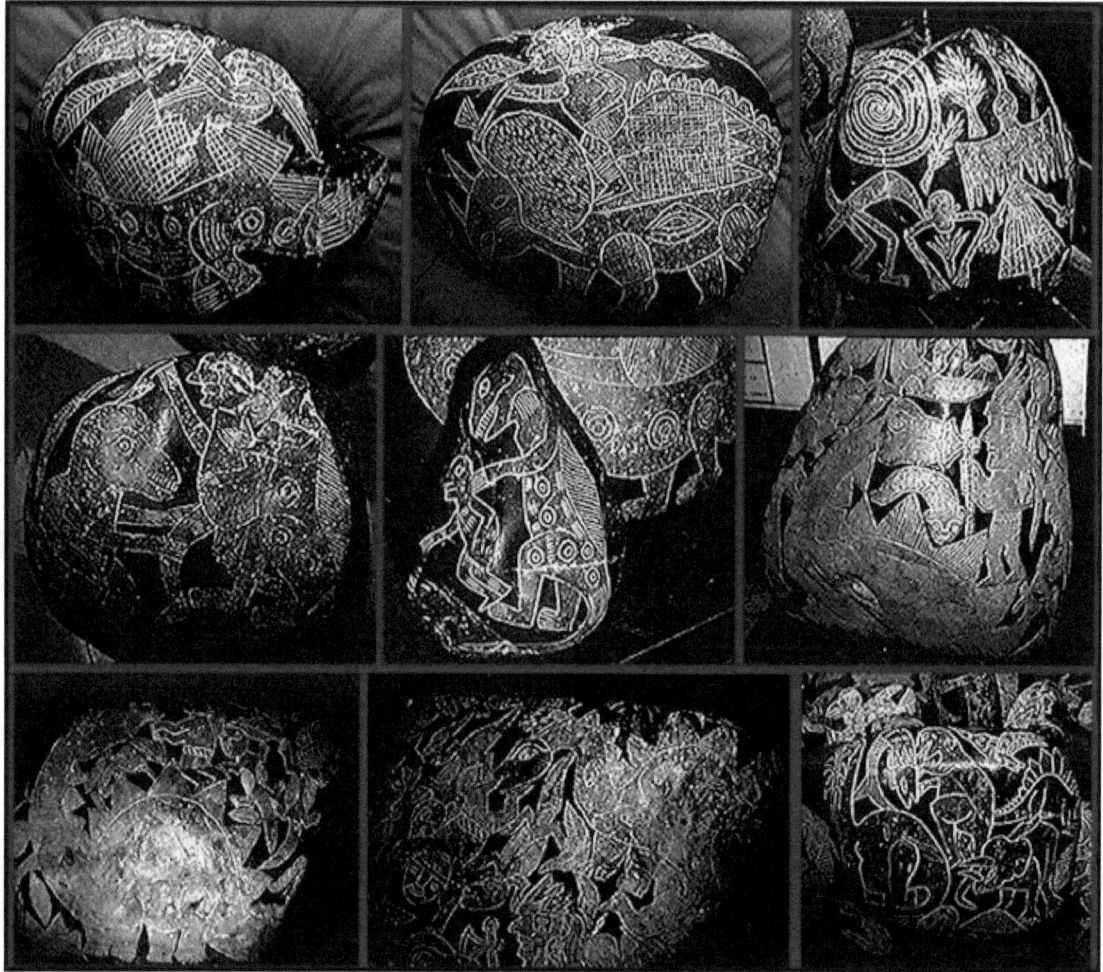

Famous Peruvian Ica Stones.

Chapter 2: Oddballs.

The mentioned aluminum-copper-platinum pendant was not the first odd archeological finding and even not the first of its kind. Thus, In China a study of the tomb of general Chou - Chzhu, killed in 297 AD, was conducted fairly recently. It showed that some elements of ornament were prepared from the alloy, into composition from copper, magnesium and aluminum. For obtaining this alloy electricity and knowledge of the process of electrolysis are required. From where it was in China in third century A.D.?

Although why not? Indeed, in the ancient men were making galvanic cells. During the archaeological excavations of the ruins city of Selevkiya in the Middle East the researchers revealed the small clay vessels with a height of 15 centimeters. In them, as reported by professor Gorbovskiy, were located iron rods and sealed copper cylinders. When electrolyte was flooded into the vessels, they gave current about 0,5-0,6 volts.

There are many other archaeological oddballs which cannot be explained by conventional science. For example, Ica stones. In 1966, Dr. Javier Cabrera, a Peruvian physician and professor of biology, was given a rock for his birthday from a local peasant. On it was a picture of an unknown fish, allegedly carved thousands of years ago. Upon further study, Cabrera realized the fish depicted was of a species that has been extinct for thousands of years. Cabrera hunted down the source of the mysterious rock and found many others like it in Ica, Peru - thousands of them and impossible ancient scenes were carved on them: telescopes, open heart surgery, flying apparatuses and even men battling dinosaurs.

In 1851, the Illinois Springfield Republican newspaper reported that a businessman named Hiram de Witt found a fist-sized chunk of auriferous quartz while on a trip to California. When it accidentally slipped from his hands, it split open, and out fell a cut-iron nail. The quartz was many thousands years old.

In 1891, Mrs. S. W. Culp, of Morrisonville, Illinois was fragmenting coal into smaller pieces for her kitchen stove when she noticed a chain stuck in the coal. The chain measured about 10 inches long and was later found to be made of eight-carat gold, and described as being "of antique and quaint workmanship." According to the Morrisonville Times of June 11, investigators concluded that the chain had not simply been accidentally dropped in with the coal, since some of the coal still clung to the chain, while the part that had separated from it still bore the impression of where the chain had been encased.

The London Times reported in 1844 that workmen quarrying stone near the River Tweed in Scotland found a piece of gold thread embedded in the rock eight feet below ground level. It was repeatedly dated to be many thousands years old.

In 1928, working the coal mines in Hiverene, Oklahoma, at a depth of about 100 meters at dismantling exploded coal found several concrete blocks. They were right cubes with all sides exactly 30 centimeters (about 1 feet). All six faces of cubes were polished smooth. Subsequent explosions of coal discovered fragments of the wall in increments of the same cubic blocks. Similar walls, only made of shale, found in 1868 the miners of coal mines in Hammondville, Ohio. On the surface of the wall can be clearly discerned a few lines hieroglyphic inscriptions.

In 1990s in deep diamond mines in South Africa, miners have found perfectly machined matching metal globes with machined ridges that run around them.

In 1991-1993, gold prospectors on the Narada river on the eastern side of the Ural mountains in Russia found unusual, mostly spiral-shaped objects, the smallest measuring about 1 / 10,000th of an inch! The objects are composed of copper and the rare metals such as tungsten and molybdenum. Tests showed the objects to be between 20,000 and 32,000 years old.

In Colombia and other Latin American countries archeologists found jewelry made from platinum, which has the melting temperature of almost 2,000 degrees Celsius (3,225 F). Those finds dated to the sixth millennium BC and earlier.

In China, they found several granite plates also containing different metals with impurities. After examining the plates, scientists concluded that they were exposed to an electric field. They were old hieroglyph like letters preserved on some plates. Scientists were able to decipher several plates text written on them, that states: «We came to this planet 12 shems (?) back. Everywhere where there is sun, there is life ».

Excavations in Peru uncovered copper coated artifacts with a thin layer of gold and silver and to make such an operations, the one must use a galvanic method, applying an electrical current. Curiously, the more ancient cultural layer, the more evidence of application of this method. By the time of Spanish conquest, these technologies have been completely lost.

Discovered on the walls of a temple in Abydos, Egypt, are hieroglyphics that very closely resemble modern aircrafts in profile: a helicopter, an airplane, and some kind of hovercraft resembling a flying disc. These hieroglyphs are still there in Abydos ancient temple.

Many pre-Columbus sculptures found in Central America made of clay and gold showing airplane flying creatures and currently displayed in museums of San Francisco, Los Angeles, New York and other major cities.

Who made those mysterious things? Clearly, not the "aliens from outer space" because of such poor assortment: nails, disks, chains, spirals, gold and clay figurines. So it is earthlings. But what civilization has left these traces?

Flying crafts found in Egyptian pyramid.

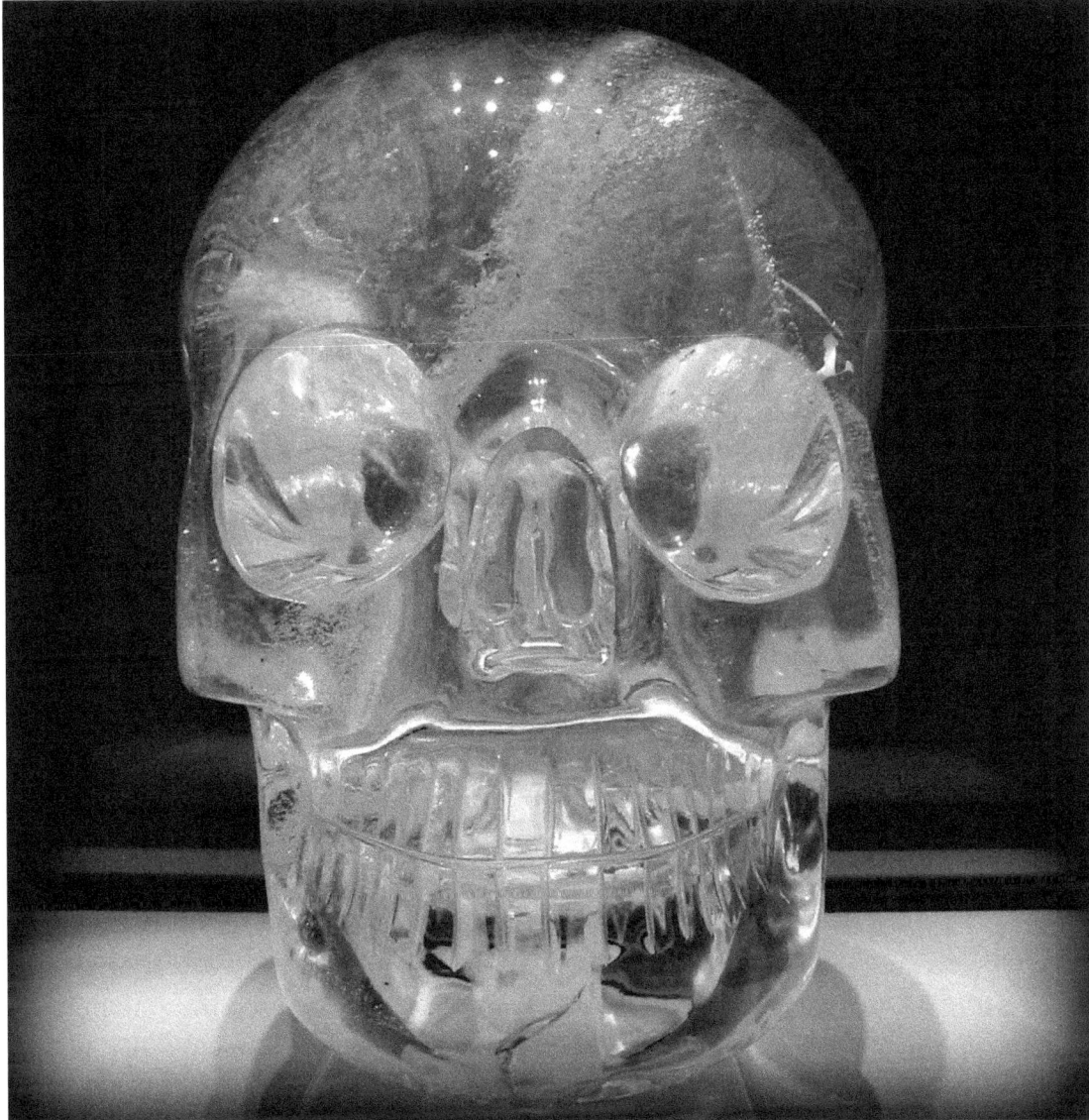
Famous crystal skull of the doom.

Chapter 3: Bogus and Real Crystal Skulls.

Crystal skulls. Unfortunately, all 12 of them after multiple careful examinations were found to be fakes made in Germany in late eighteen and early nineteen century. Including two beautiful fakes displayed by British National museum for over a century as real pre-Columbus South American skulls of the doom. However, the thirteenth skull is reaming a real enigma. It was unearthed recently in Honduras, in the small city Lubaantum. Archeologists were shocked by its beauty and perfection of this rock crystal skull. The skull also has an impossible geometry and very unusual cutting techniques unlike those used to create known German duplicates. Yes, it is possible to recreate such skull today but only in the high tech lab using 21st century equipment assuming that you find the right 20 lbs piece of rock crystal and it won't break during the process. But most of archeologist agree - it could not be cut in Honduras with such precision neither in 19th nor in 20th century. It is seems obvious that another real crystal skull did exist and unknown German master, who was mass producing its replicas, was well aware of its existence but none of his neatly crafted replicas did not have the quality of the original.

The other famous bogus artifact is "Spark plug" in a geode. In 1961, the owners of a gift shop in Olancha, California found a fossil-encrusted geode in the Coso Mountains. When one of the owners cut the geode in half with a diamond saw, he found an object inside that was obviously artificial. The object had a metal core surrounded by layers of a ceramic-like material and a hexagonal wooden sleeve. It had been completely encased in a geode that was covered with fossils estimated to be 500,000 years old. When X-rayed, the object seemed to resemble a modern spark plug with some other electronic component from Ford model T - obvious forgery.

The same way, in June, 1851, Scientific American magazine reprinted a report from the Boston Transcript about how a metallic vase found in two parts was dynamited out of solid rock 15 feet below the surface in Dorchester, Mass. The bell-shaped vase, measuring 4-1/2 inches high and 6-1/2 inches at the base, was composed of a zinc and silver alloy. On the sides were figures of flowers in bouquet arrangements, inlaid with pure silver. The estimated age of the rock out of which it came: 1 million years. It was saved an re-examined in late 20th century and researches find out that vase was not that old at all.

Because of human stupidity some priceless artifacts will never reveal us their true nature. Thus, an illiterate Peruvian farmer discovered more than ten thousand unique artifacts in the form of stones of various sizes on which the ancient artist had engraved absolutely unbelievable scenes: such as previously mentioned engaging in battles with the dinosaurs, sitting at the telescope, performing complex surgical procedures, flying disks, etc. In order not to change history of the evolution of mankind, "the pillars of science" publicly announced these phenomenal artifacts as forgery, throw farmer into prison for allegedly tampering with them, and destroyed nearly all 10,000 stones.

Here is another typical example of handling non-scientific evidence, which contradicts to conventional plans. These events associated with finds of mysterious mummies in desert So-La-Makan, West China. Anthropologists have identified rare finds: type of people belonging to some not previously known tribe. They were Caucasian people who populated that land even before the first imperial dynasty in China. They were white-headed, blue-eyed people who wore beautiful colorful bright clothes and shoes. This discovery brought a tide of optimism but neither scientists, nor the authorities could not give proper answers, and they decided to give it a little publicity, and not to turn layers of history or rewrite the history, the mysterious burial just ... buried back to earth.

However, mounting evidence of real artifacts already made conventional science to step back and re-write some its dogmas. Thus, I had learned in school that humans started using fire about 100,000 years ago but the new widely accepted theory now printed in text books says that humans had the ability to make fire nearly 800,000 years ago, a skill that helped them migrate from Africa to Europe. A lot of new irrefutable evidence in the pre historic caves was found and fire timeline shifted at least 700,000 years into the past.

My ancient history textbook said that humans started to wear furs and skins of dead animals about 35,000 years ago when the Great Ice Age has arrived. About 25,000 years ago they started to wear primitive shoes as well. However, multiple new excavations suggest that humans started wearing shoes about 50,000 years ago, and clothes were found dated to 80 thousands years BC. That is over 40 thousands years earlier than previously thought. And not only the primitive but some very well made shoes were found fit to walk in a cold weather much better than modern Nikes. As saying goes "As any good clothes horse knows, the right outfit speaks volumes about the person wearing it." Now, anthropologists are tapping into that knowledge base, looking for the physical changes caused by wearing shoes to figure out when footwear first became fashionable. Turns out, "clothes really do make the man." So the official anthropology admits that it was misguided by 30,000 to 700,000 years in some questions, what's other surprises are waiting to be unearthed?

Mysterious vase found in coal.

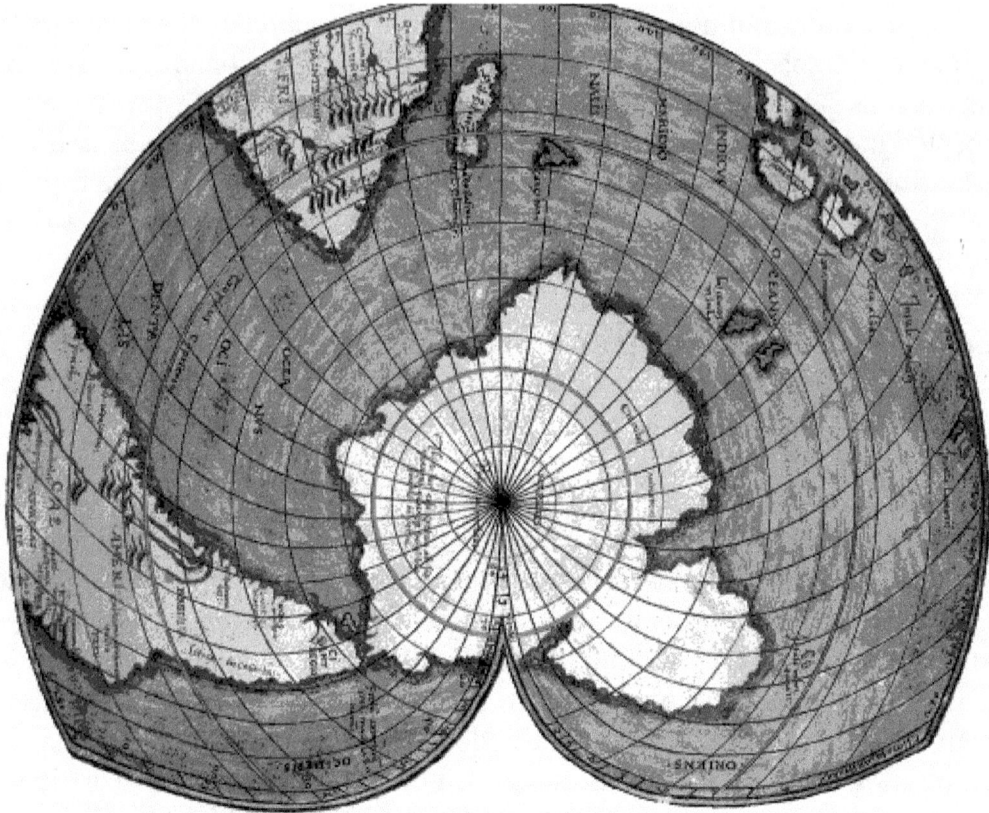
Medieval Antarctica map drawn from ancient sources.

Chapter 4: Antarctica Maps.

In January 1820 Lieutenant of Russian emperor fleet Mikhail Petrovich Lazarev discovered a new continent on the map of our planet: Antarctica. The known Russian encyclopedic dictionary of Brockhaus at the beginning of present century already reported that the south-polar continent was insufficiently studied; flora and fauna seems to be absent. It indicated the approximate estimation of the area of continent as well. Also the contributor noted wealth of Antarctic waters by algae and by marine animals.

However, in the National Museum of Turkey you will find on display two map fragments dated 1513 and 1528. The maps were compiled from a number of now lost ancient originals which existed long before the time of the Greeks. At the bottom of one of these fragments is shown the coastline of much of the Antarctic continent, including rivers and mountains. The original map, which demonstrates amazing knowledge and accuracy, was made when Antarctica was ice-free. Antarctic mountains and portions of the coastline depicted on the map were confirmed by scientific studies in 1952 and again more recently. The evidence of the maps can't be ignored, according to responsible reviewers who have studied them (Hapgood, 1966). Officially, Antarctic ice cap is 60,000,000 years old, while some new theories suggest that Antarctic cup melted and freeze several times but we are still talking about at least tens of thousands of years.

After twenty years since Lazarev's new continent discovery the director of national museum in Istanbul by Halil Edkhem investigated the library of Byzantine emperors in the old palace of sultans. Here, on the dusty shelf, it revealed the map, which was made on the skin of deer and convoluted into a tube. Map compiler depicted on it the western shore of Africa, the South coast of South America and the northern shore of Antarctica. Halil did not believe his eyes. Coast edge of Queen Land south of the 70th parallel was free from ice. Compiler also applied in this place the existing mountain range. The name of compiler is well known - Admiral of the fleet of Ottoman empire and cartographer Peary Reis, who lived in first half XVI of century - three hundreds years before the Antarctica official discovery.

The authenticity of map did not cause doubts. The grapho-logical examination of side notes confirmed that they were performed by the hand of Turkish Admiral. Besides, Peary Reis himself explained in the side notes, comprised at the beginning XVI of century, that he does not bear any responsibility for primary survey and cartography, and its map is based on a large quantity of earlier sources. Some of them are drawn by its contemporaries (for example, by Christopher Columbus), while the others relate to the older times and can be dated by pre-Christian era and some belonged to Alexander The Great Macedonian, who lived in that epoch.

Joint British-Swedish research expedition made extensive seismic exploration for the southernmost continent through the thick ice cover. According to the commander of the 8th squadron of technical intelligence Strategic Command United States Air Force (from 06.07.1960) Lieutenant Colonel Harold Z. Olmeyer "geographical details are displayed in the bottom of the card (the coast of Antarctica - VA), perfectly consistent with the seismic survey data … We can not imagine how to reconcile the data that maps to the level of geographical science in 1513. "

That's not all - in 1959 professor of Kinský College (New Hampshire, US), Charles H. Hepgud found another Antarctica map at the Library of Congress in Washington drawn up by Oronteusom Finius. Dating drawing - the year of 1531 AD. Oronteus Finius depicted Antarctica with ice-free beaches, mountains and rivers. The terrain of central part of the continent is indicated that, in the opinion of professor Hepgud suggest the presence in the ice cap in the center of the continent.

Later research of Finius map by Massachusetts Institute of Technology, Dr. Richard Streychan revealed that O. Finius really showing the ice-free coast of Antarctica. The general shape and characteristics of the terrain is very similar to those reported for the hidden beneath the ice surface of the mainland, which were mapped in early 1960s by specialists from different countries (including the USA and USSR).

Gerard Kremer, known worldwide under the name of Mercator, also included a map in so-called Finius atlas which had several maps of Antarctica. In addition, there is one interesting feature on the Mercator map, drawn up in 1569: west coast of South America shown less accurate than the earlier map of the Mercator in 1538. The reasons for this contradiction as follows: when working on an early map cartographer XVI century based on more accurate ancient sources, which did not reach us, and later on the map - the observations and measurements of the first Spanish researchers west of South America. Error of Gerard Mercator is excusable because in the XVI century there were no accurate methods of measuring longitude and, as a result, the error amounted to hundreds of kilometers.

Medieval maps show Antarctica without ice cover or ice cover partially preserving. The accuracy of mapping assessments XVI century is very high and on a number of positions surprising. These figures exceed the technical capacity of even the late Middle Ages (the definition of longitude of relief up to a minute). In the best case, this level of engineering of our humanity in line with the first part of nineteen century, and on many issues (such as under ice relief) - just the middle of the last century. Who was the source of the original accurate maps drawn millennia ago?

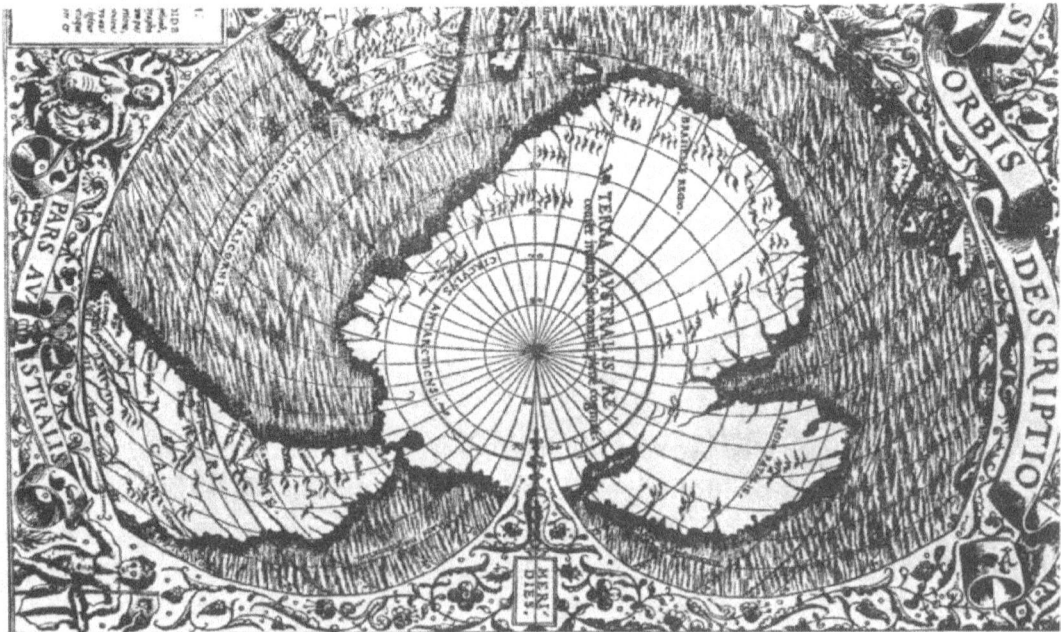

Oronteusom Finius Antarctica map of 1531 AD.

Ancient Greek Antikythera Computer.

Chapter 5: Ancient Technology.

In 1901, an ancient clock-like mechanism surfaced off the coast of the Greek island of Antikythera. The original 1959 Scientific American Magazine article on the device called it "the most complex scientific object that has been preserved from antiquity." The Antikythera Computer, as it is now called, had apparently been used to calculate the position of the stars as an aid to navigation. This computer predates the supposed invention of clockwork gears by millennia and is still considered only a curiosity by mainstream science. However, it is unlikely that the only one Greek computer ever built would have been preserved, so presumably there were others so-called Antikythera Celestial Machines.

Many sources comment on the exquisite workmanship of ancient artifacts. There have been rumors of archaic vessels made out of platinum or aluminum, metals not used in the West until the nineteenth century. Unfortunately, most of these objects seem to exist only in the pages of yellow press and are nearly always described as "missing" or "lost" or "stolen". Consequently, it is impossible to comment on the veracity of most claims of ancient metallurgy, but an analysis of the remains of metal clamps used to hold together the blocks of the ancient Andean city of Tihuanaco seems to imply that the alloy used a much higher smelting temperature than most archaeologists believe Andean peoples could generate.

Here is another well known example. Despite nearly a century of theorizing, no one has been able to certainly determine how ancient people moved the massive megaliths that make up ancient buildings. Such structures seem to defy attempts to explain them. While many competent theories have been proposed (and many more incompetent ones), no one can claim to completely solve the mystery of the megaliths building and movement.

At Ollantaytambo, to take one example, there are series of polygonal megaliths weighing upwards of 70 to 100 metric tons each are fitted together in an immense jigsaw puzzle of a wall over 260 feet tall. What makes this more amazing, is that all of the immense stones had been transported 195 feet up the side of a mountain from a quarry located five miles away and almost 3,000 feet higher on the other end of the Vilcamayu river valley.

Other megalithic sites of the same order include Sacsayhuaman, Tihuanaco, the Great Pyramid, and scattered ruins on the beautiful Polynesian islands. Other megalithic sites of large scale include Easter Island, Stonehenge, Carnak and the inexplicable stone spheres of Costa Rica. These spheres are near-perfectly spherical and range in size from an inch to tens of feet in diameter. They are placed seemingly at random across the jungles of Central America and, though we know how they were made, their purpose has never been satisfactorily explained.

The "embryological disc" is one of the most interesting pieces from South America. The front and back show relief-type image symbols. One thesis states that they show the evolution from an amphibian to a human. Medical experts agree: Decisive developmental stages of human life can be identified. These features are characteristic for an early embryonic structure. But from what time is the disc? Geologists at the University of Bogotá date it to a prehistoric epoch. The most recent examinations were unable to find evidence of faking. Could the strange find come from a lost advanced culture? Was their knowledge equal to ours?

At 17,000 years old, the unusual Nomoli figure from West Africa is also considered the oldest even by convention science. A small metal ball was hidden in a hollow space inside it. An analysis showed that it is made from chrome and steel. However, the metal ball was already in the figure when it was found. How did it get there? And much more important - where did the metal come from? The blue "Skystones" from the same region are another mystery. A legend says: "The part of the sky in which the Nomoli lived turned to stone. It splintered and fell to Earth as pieces of rock." Scientists found iridium in the "Skystones". However, there is no iridium on Earth, unless it was brought in from space by a meteorite, asteroid or some other means.

Electrical power in ancient Egypt? We find indicators of this in the Hathor temple of Dendera in Egypt. Relieves show insulator-like columns. They support large, long structures in which wave like snakes are shown. What is baffling is that the depictions show an exact similarity to depictions of electrical discharges. Surprisingly, the texts of Dendera also contain technical data and segments which can be linked with the electricity hypothesis. In 1981, the Viennese electrical expert Walter Garn constructed this functional model in accordance with the Pharaoh models. But are ancient tales of "eternally burning lamps" really the stuff of legends?

Many primitive people tell how heavenly gods visited and taught their ancestors. This is how the Dogon tribe from the republic of Mali know astronomic details of the Sirius system. Their holy sign of iron shows the orbits of the stars Sirius B and C. Strange - the white dwarf Sirius B can only be seen with a very powerful telescope. And modern astronomy determined details only in the last century. According to our current knowledge, Sirius B takes 50 years to complete one revolution around Sirius A. Surprisingly, the Dogon have celebrated the Sirius system regularly every 50 years for generations. This is where their gods, the Nommos, are said to live. With the four meter high Sirigi masks, they imitate the landing of the gods' ark on Earth.

Modern Working Model of Ancient Greek Celestial Machine.

Electrical light bulb found in Egyptian Pyramid.

Chapter 6: Different Continents - Same Stories.

Still on the roster of unsolved mysteries is the question of just how much contact ancient cultures had with one another. Recently the story of the Egyptian cocaine mummies has reopened questions long thought answered. Analysis of Egyptian mummies has turned up traces of cocaine in hair follicles, implying that the Ancient Egyptians chewed coca leaves, a plant found only on the continent of South America.

The United States has had many cases of mysterious stones and markers bearing writing variously attributed to Phonecians, Egyptians, Vikings and Celts. While the vast majority of these are obviously racist hoaxes designed to bolster Euro-American claims to Native American lands, at least a handful of these artifacts have not been explained. In addition, late twentieth-century research confirmed that Vikings had colonized a portion of eastern Canada, the famous Vineland, during the eleventh century.

An archaeological team announced in 2001 that coins with very close resemblance to Roman had been discovered underneath the floor of an Aztec temple, proving that Roman goods had been present in the New World before Columbus. This based on reports of a Roman-style sculpture discovered in Mexico and Roman amphorae in Brazil. While some of these goods could have arrived through ships blown off course or by conquistadors bringing a bit of home with them, this mystery remains unexplained.

Almost all early civilizations had the same myth - called Great Flood Story. Who told them about the Great Ancient Tsunami?

It is generally accepted that the era of "flying saucers" has started in the middle of XX century, when American businessmen Kenneth Arnold, who went on a plane to search for a missing friend, was watching a few unidentified objects moving in the sky. In fact, the past century, only confirmed abnormal phenomena observed by people throughout history. Robert Nelson (after study and comparative analysis of numerous historical documents) concluded that the mysterious objects, and the mysterious substances, called at different times by different names (gods, angels, demons, flying chariots, fire dragons, shining the birds, aliens, aliens, interplanetary ships), were in contact with humankind throughout history. Maybe they are and have become the creators of this history and, perhaps, humans. Myths of almost all ancient people tell us about "gods descended from heaven" to teach people crafts, give them different knowledge, teach to build the temples, show how to meliorate the land. In the stories described how the gods gave people «the wisdom and understanding» and bestowed on them from heaven «royal power». According to the ancient Sumerians, the gods, not only lived on earth, but also to travel to the heavens, where lived the great goddess-mother. They are used for the «wonderful shiny birds» for those heaven trips.

Legends of the ancient Inca report that their god Ketsalkoatl descended to the ground in the "sparkling boat that could, like a bird, soaring in the air and move through the water without the aid of oar together with the profit of 19 satellites." Ketsalkoatl measured the land, taught ancient Indian mathematics and astronomy, has opened useful plants, has taught people to use fire, to build homes and to live as husband and wife.

In Egyptian mythology «gods descended to Earth in ancient times from heaven. God Ra was the first god and master, and the ruled 300,000 years ». God Ra ruled together with his brothers and Tóth and Set who «knew heaven, could count the stars, enumerate all that is on earth, and measure the Earth». The gods also taught to cultivate the land, to live in peace, to manage and educate their children.

Japanese, Chinese, Mongolian and Tibetan myths also tell us about «sons of heaven», which came down from heaven to live on Earth. Traditions and myths extremely similar, indicating that they all describe the actual events that took place in ancient times.

Most religions have the belief that there was once a more perfect world, from which man has been banished. This has often been interpreted as a meaning of a real previous powerful civilization used to exist, populated by beings who were seen as gods by ancient humans.

Egyptian Sphinx.

Chapter 7: Knowledge Transfer.

There is a version that tens of thousands years ago there was a civilization has reached an unprecedented level of development. Along with this powerful civilization Earth was inhabited by the ancestors of modern humans. As it is now, for example, along with modern humans, there are Australian pygmies and African and South American tribes living in the Stone Age. At some point in its development a powerful civilization or destroyed itself (we have such ability too), or it was the victim of natural cataclysm. The population of the planet due to the techno-genic or natural disaster was drastically reduced, and that forced the representatives of a highly developed civilization to contact the «primitive» people whom they had not taken seriously before. It is possible that our ancestors saw the them, with their unseen knowledge and technical means, as gods and worshiped them. So did and primitive tribes of the Americas, and even the Incas and the Maya, when Spanish colonizers stepped on their land.

Anthropologists from various countries show that the «primitive people» tend to see the gods in more developed nations, and to imitate what they have seen. History knows many examples when the missionaries, conquerors, travelers, and ordinary people are taken by the various tribes for the gods and supreme beings. The most glaring example - Spanish conquistadors, when the local tribes have thought the gods and did not resist the conquerors. Similarly, in 1871, Russian traveler Miklukho-Maklay come to the shores of New Guinea. Local people took him for the supreme god Anut that «with the other white gods came down from the Moon at the great divine vessel».

Furthermore, in 1945, on a small island Vivak in the Pacific Ocean a strange religious cult was developed. For a long time Aborigines watched different planes, which landed on their island and then rocket into the sky. When the island's airstrip has been moved to another location and aircrafts no longer arrive to Vivak, Aborigines have been making huge models airplanes out of straw, leafs and grass, hoping that «celestial birds will come again».

The Dutch soldiers, who were based on the island of New Guinea, noted the remarkable feature of native people. Observing Dutch troops, they began to construct vehicles and radio stations from straw and leaves. Aborigines also talked with each other using wooden microphones, using carved wooden dishes for reception, and twisted the leaves in the form of capacitors.

Such examples show that the primitive people copying unclear to them technology, and adapting more advanced nations devices using primitive means such as leafs, straw or stone. From the point of view of ethnologists, sociologists and anthropologists, there is no doubt that in ancient times, people have also taken over the gods of any superior creatures, copying their clothing, equipment, behavior, etc. Science can not answer yet who were these mysterious aliens or newcomers in ancient times.

Center to such ideas is Atlantis, an mythical land deep in our past with a perfect, but powerful society, finally destroyed by the gods when they were corrupted. From 12,000 to 9,000 BC, the last Ice Age ended, raising water levels. Hence, these communities were wiped out, leaving only enigmatic structures poking up from the sea bed, the survivors going inland and using their expertise which was repeated and copied all over the world. These survivors are remembered only as gods. And the first global society that rose to greatness was finally wiped off the face of the Earth.

Very unusual Lonar crater in India.

Chapter 8: Ancient Nukes.

Incredible as it may seem, archaeologists have found considerable evidence in India and Pakistan, indicating that cities there were destroyed in atomic explosions. "When excavations of Harappa and Mohenjo-Daro reached the street level, they discovered skeletons scattered about the cities, many holding hands and sprawling in the streets as if some instant, horrible doom had taken place. People were just lying, unburied, in the streets of the city. And these skeletons are many thousands of years old, tested according to traditional archaeological standards. What could cause such a thing? Furthermore, there is no apparent cause of a physically violent death.

These skeletons are among the most radioactive ever found, such as those at Nagasaki and Hiroshima. At one site, Soviet scholars found skeletons which had a radioactive level 50 times greater than normal.

The Russian archaeologist A. Gorbovsky mentions the high incidence of radiation associated with the skeletons in his 1966 book, Riddles of Ancient History. Furthermore, many thousands of fused lumps, christened "black stones", have been found at Mohenjo-Daro. These appear to be fragments of clay vessels that melted together in extreme heat.

Other cities have been found in northern India that show indications of explosions of great magnitude. One such city, found between the Ganges and the mountains of Rajmahal, seems to have been subjected to intense heat. Huge masses of walls and foundations of the ancient city are fused together, literally vitrified! And since there is no indication of a volcanic eruption at Mohenjo-Daro or at the other cities, the intense heat to melt clay vessels can only be explained by an atomic blast or some other unknown weapon. The cities were wiped out entirely.

If we accept the Lemurian fellowship stories as fact, then Atlantis wanted to waste no more time with the Priest-Kings of Rama and their tricks. In terrifying revenge, they utterly destroyed the Rama Empire, leaving no country even to pay tribute to them. The areas around the cities of Harappa and Mohenjo-Daro have also been desolated in the past, though agriculture takes place to a limited extent in the vicinity today.

It is said in esoteric literature that Atlantis at the same time, or shortly afterwards, also attempted to subjugate a civilization extant in the area of the Gobi Desert, which was then a fertile plain. By using some mysterious weaponry, they wiped out their adversaries as well.

Much speculation naturally exists in connection with remote history. We may never actually know the complete truth, though ancient texts still in existence are certainly a good start.

Atlantis met its own doom, according to Plato, by sinking into the ocean in a mighty cataclysm-not too long after the war with the Rama Empire. Kashmir is also connected with the fantastic war that destroyed the Rama Empire in ancient times. The massive ruins of a temple called Parshaspur can be found just outside Srinagar. It is a scene of total destruction. Huge blocks of stone are scattered about a wide area, giving the impression of explosive annihilation. Was Parshaspur destroyed by some fantastic weapon during one of the horrendous battles detailed in the *Mahabharata*?

Another curious sign of an ancient nuclear war in India is a giant crater near Bombay. The nearly circular 2,154-meter-diameter (almost 1.5 miles) Lonar crater, located 400 kilometres northeast of Bombay and aged at less than 30,000 years old, could be related to nuclear warfare of antiquity. No trace of any meteoric material, etc., has been found at the site or in the vicinity, and this is the world's only known "impact" crater in basalt. Indications of great shock (from a pressure exceeding 600,000 atmospheres) and intense, abrupt heat (indicated by basalt glass spherules) can be ascertained from the site.

Conventional science cannot, of course, concede nuclear possibilities for such craters, even in the absence of any material meteorite or related evidence. If such geologically recent craters as the Lonar are of meteoric origin, then why it also show higher then normal level of radioactivity? A theory was advanced by American space consultant Pat Frank, to the effect that some of the huge craters on the Earth may be scars from ancient nuclear explosions!

The echoes of ancient atomic warfare in southern Asia continue to this day, with India and Pakistan currently threatening each other. Modern India is proud of its nukes, likening them to "Rama's Arrow". Similarly, Pakistan would to use its Islamic atomic bombs on India but retaliation fear stops both sides so far. Ironically, Kashmir, possibly the site of an earlier atomic war, is the focus of this conflict. Will the past repeat itself in Pakistan and India? There is always the possibility that this has all happened before. *Déjà vu!*"

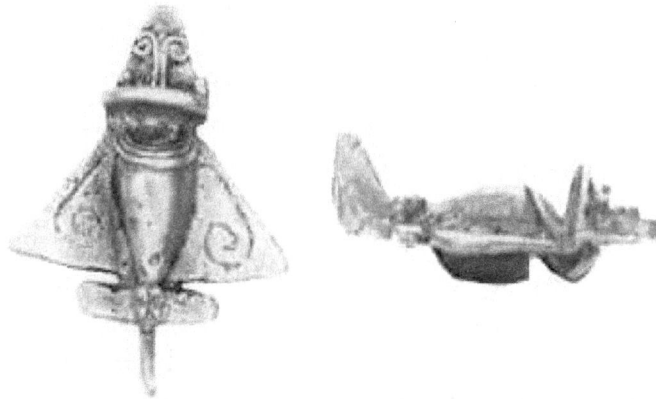

Gold Ancient Aircraft from Colombian National Museum.

Dinosaur in ancient Cambodian temple.

Chapter 9: Missing Link.

According to the book "Forbidden Archeology - The Hidden History of the Human Race" by Michael A. Cremo and Richard L. Thompson following events took place. In the 1950s, Louis Leakey found stone tools over 200,000 years old at Calico in southern California. According to standard views, humans did not enter the sub arctic regions of the New World until about 12,000 years ago. Mainstream scientists responded to Calico with predictable claims that the objects found there were natural products or that they were not really 200,000 years old. But there is sufficient reasons to conclude that the Calico finds are genuinely old human artifacts. Although most of the Calico implements are crude, some, including a beaked graver, are more advanced.

In the early 1950s, Thomas E. Lee of the National Museum of Canada found advanced stone tools in glacial deposits at Sheguiandah, on Manitoulin Island in northern Lake Huron. Geologist John Sanford of Wayne State University argued that the oldest Sheguiandah tools from at least 65,000 years old and to as much as 125,000 years old. For those adhering to standard views on North American prehistory, such ages were unacceptable.

Furthermore, in the category of crude paleoliths, we include Miocene tools (5 million years old) found in the late nineteenth century by Carlos Ribeiro, head of the Geological Survey of Portugal. At an international conference of archeologists and anthropologists held in Lisbon, a committee of scientists investigated one of the sites where Ribeiro had found implements. One of the scientists found a stone tool even more advanced than the better of Ribeiro's specimens. Comparable to accepted Late Pleistocene tools of the Mousterian type, it was firmly embedded in a Miocene conglomerate, in circumstances confirming its Miocene antiquity.

Carlos Ameghino, brother of Florentino Ameghino, carried out new investigations at Miramar, on the Argentine coast south of Buenos Aires. There he found a series of stone implements, including bolas, and signs of fire. A commission of geologists confirmed the implements' position in the Chapadmalalan formation, which modern geologists say is 3 million years old. Carlos Ameghino also found at Miramar a stone arrowhead firmly embedded in the femur of a Pliocene species of *Toxodon,* an extinct South American mammal.

This pattern of data suppression has a long history. In 1880, J. D. Whitney, the state geologist of California, published a lengthy review of advanced stone tools found in California gold mines. The implements, including spear points and stone mortars and pestles, were found deep in mine shafts, underneath thick, undisturbed layers of lava, in formations that geologists now say are millions years old. Some of them are still stored at UC Berkley.

Now we can, finally, draw the full picture. Contrary to the conventional science human like apes either appear or come to America millions of years ago. Thus, it was proven and written by conventional science that: Australopithecus shared several traits with modern apes and humans, and were widespread throughout Eastern and Northern Africa by a time between 4.0 and 3.0 million years ago. The earliest evidence of fundamentally bipedal hominids can be observed at the site of Laetoli in Tanzania. This site contains hominid footprints that are remarkably similar to those of modern humans and have been dated to as old as 3.9 million years. Until recently, the footprints have generally been classified as Australopithecus because that had been the only form of pre-human known to have existed in that region at that time; however, some scholars have considered reassigning them to a yet unidentified very early species of the genus Homo." Actually accepting that primitive humans like apes existed in Australia over 3 million years ago and used tools and fire and they were probably branch of Orrorin or Sahelanthropus who existed around the time of the split in Africa between 6 and 7 million years BC, and who also may be ancestral to both humans and chimpanzees. The question remain, who did australopiths ended up in isolated continent of Australia?

Their missing American relatives (Ameropithetecus) whose bones were found in America and well described by many scientists but never officially classified first started to use very primitive tools about the same time or even earlier 4 millions years ago or more.

Ancient Egyptian Elongated Heads Sculptures.

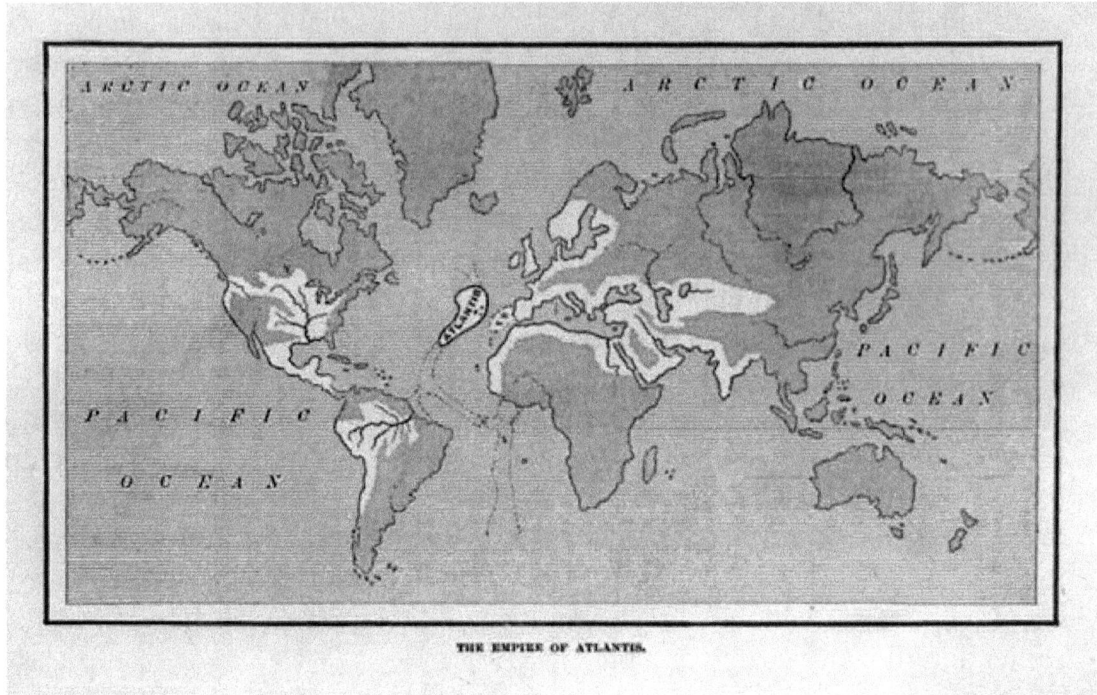

THE EMPIRE OF ATLANTIS.

19th century Atlantis map.

Chapter 10: Atlantis: Plato Story.

In 2003 while studying biology in SFSU I heard from another professor who told his students that although ancient humans were genetically identical to modern humans and there was no obstacles in bearing healthy children if sexual intercourse between modern and ancient humans was possible. True. But he also added that first human civilizations appeared only about 5,000 years ago and humans used their genotype to transform into a different phenotype (real life realization of your genes) than modern humans do before 3,000 BC (like instead of stressing on social and building skills developing hunting and gathering skills). The lesson was not in the form of a lecture but more in in form of a discussion so I objected and said that there are some proofs that earlier civilization or civilizations have existed. He said that there is no such proofs of earlier civilizations ever existed and that Egypt and Mesopotamia were the first organized societies and scientifically confirmed by massive finding of their artifacts. He questioned me in front of the class asking maybe Mr. Kryan will explain us why we cannot not see these mysterious Atlantis artifacts. He did not wait for my answer and answered to his own questions: "We cannot see them because they do not exist as well as Atlantis did not exist." Then, I replied to his question (my reply cost me the whole grade. I got B for the course instead of a well deserved A). I told the students: "Do you see professor's brains? No. So according to professor, if we cannot see them they also do not exist." But looks like we can find more or less solid proofs of "mysterious Atlantis artifacts" after all.

Legends of lost continents like Atlanits, Lemuria and Mu aside, tantalizing remains of underwater architecture still remain unexplained. Among the most prominent submarine ruins is the famous Bimini Road, discovered in 1968. This miles-long complex of stonework that resembles a road or the walls of buildings is officially classified as a natural formation, but some scientist believe that the arrow-straight lines and right-angle turns imply an artificial source. Divers also report that patterns formed by the stones loosely resemble the ground plans of Mayan temples.

On the other side of the world, Nan Madol is one of the great stone structures on earth. Its basalt megaliths form temples, palaces and other buildings with upturned corners so that they resemble boats. The native people remember legends that beneath the original Nan Madol, down in the ocean, is the primeval Nan Madol built during the glorious reign of the gods. Great stone pillars of this ancient city can still be seen off the island of Ponape.

Off the southernmost island of Japan, the Yonaguni Monument has created a heated controversy because of its resemblance to megalithic temples in South America and the Pacific islands. Japanese researchers have declared the structure man-made about 9,000 BC while some American scientists say Yonaguni is a natural formation. Both parties have strong arguments but the underwater mysteries remain unexplained.

In ancient Greek philosopher and historian Plato's account, Atlantis was a naval power lying "beyond of the Pillars of Hercules" that conquered many parts of Western Europe and Africa 9,000 years before the time of Solon, or approximately 9,700 BC sank into the ocean "in a single day and night of misfortune" on the day they were preparing to invade what is now the modern Greece. Their island, army and fleet sank as well as the whole army of primitive Greeks defenders according to Plato.

This legendary island is first mentioned in Plato's dialogues *Timaeus* and *Critias*: "For it is related in our records how once upon a time your State stayed the course of a mighty host, which, starting from a distant point in the Atlantic ocean, was insolently advancing to attack the whole of Europe, and Asia to boot. For the ocean there was at that time navigable; for in front of the mouth which you Greeks call, as you say, 'the pillars of Heracles,' there lay an island which was larger than Libya and Asia together; and it was possible for the travelers of that time to cross from it to the other islands, and from the islands to the whole of the continent over against them which encompasses that veritable ocean. For all that we have here, lying within the mouth of which we speak, is evidently a haven having a narrow entrance; but that yonder is a real ocean, and the land surrounding it may most rightly be called, in the fullest and truest sense, a continent. Now in this island of Atlantis there existed a confederation of kings, of great and marvelous power, which held sway over all the island, and over many other islands also and parts of the continent."

Plato also say's that Egypt was ruled by the first dynasty of god-like pharaohs for tens of thousands years. The Egyptians, Plato asserted, described Atlantis as an island comprising mountains in the northern portions and along the shore, and encompassing great plains of an oblong shape in the south. The Egyptians were in contact Atlantis for millennia according to their own sources and another well known ancient historian Herodotus.

Ancient aircrafts made from gold from Colombia museum.

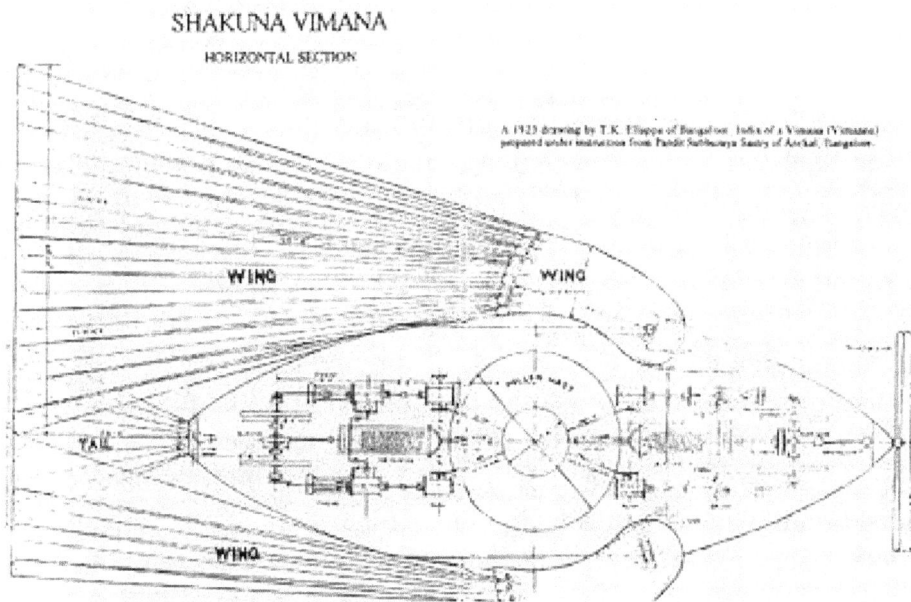

SHAKUNA VIMANA

HORIZONTAL SECTION

A 1923 drawing by T.K. Ellappa of Bangalore, India of a Vimana (Vimaana) prepared under instructions from Pandit Subbaraya Sastry of Anekal, Bangalore.

WING   WING

TAIL

WING

Drawings done in 1923 from the vimana texts.

Ancient Indian Flying Vessel.

Chapter 11: Atlantis. The Real Story.

We may never know how Australopithecus end up in Australia and why they disappeared or evolved into modern Australia pygmies but now we have some ideas about their missing American relatives (Ameropithetecus). A little doubt that the same species who give to Australopithecus (Orrorin or Sahelanthropus) were also ancestors of Ameropithetecus. We cannot explain how the primitive human like apes sailed to Australia but we can guess that Orrorin or Sahelanthropus migrated to America from Africa though Asia which were more or less interconnected in the north. Even conventional science tells us that Orrorin or Sahelanthropus first appeared almost 7 million years ago so it is not that hard to estimate that 1 million of years would enough time for their migration to America. In other worlds - these humanoid apes were in North America by 6 million BC and spread to central and south America by 5 million BC branching into a separate species which we call Ameropithetecus. It is fair to estimate that migration from Africa have continued for at least 6 millions years insuring good genetic flow both ways between Africa, Eurasia and Americas.

From American archeological findings described earlier it is clear that Ameropithethecus became much more advanced than his African, Australian and Eurasian relatives. Time to time Ameropithecus become separated from the rest of the world because of repeating Ice Ages which were closing genetic flow and allowing these hominids to evolve into the first humans, who spread to the rest of the world before the previous greatest Ice Age that occurred about 650 thousand years ago and lasted 50,000 years. During this period the ice advanced deep into the Midwest, from its center around Hudson Bay in Canada and covered all of Siberia and most of the Europe making Eurasia-America passage impossible and completely cutting off humanity in America.

During that time most of North American continent and as well as part of South America was under ice and snow. It was much cooler and worse conditions than during the latest famous Great Ice Age 40,000 BC - 10,000 BC so American part of humanity had three choices: adapt, migrate closer to Equator (to Mexican deserts and treacherous jungles of South America) or die out. By analyzing the tools of that period it is apparent that North American people choose to adapt: mastered fire techniques, invented clothes, learned to build houses, created advanced hunting and survival techniques, made stone knifes and spears in order to survive. This gave them the huge advantage comparatively to the rest of the world - they evolved into the first true humans and acquired first ancient technologies.

By the time the well known Great Ice Age was fully blown or about 30,000 BC ancient American people became the first real civilization known to Plato as Atlantis. They inhibited both North and South America. Indeed, Plato says "a naval power lying far beyond of the Pillars of Hercules" (known as beginning of Atlantic ocean - beyond Gibraltar strait between West Africa and Spain) and their land was bigger than Libya (Plato actually means whole known Africa) and Asia (Plato means known to him Middle East) combined and an island comprising mountains in the northern portions and along the shore, and encompassing great plains of an oblong shape in the south with many surrounding islands. There is only one land mass fitting this description - Americas.

Atlantis became the mightiest and unrivaled power on earth tens of thousands years ago. For most of their flourishing times Atlantes prefer not to spread to other continents having enough resources in Americas. By 9,700 BC or 12,000 year ago they definitely know how to produce electricity, achieved very high level of metallurgy, built flying aircrafts, large ships and, perhaps, even mastered nuclear power. In other worlds, they achieved technical level of at least 19th century and, perhaps, even mid 20th century - surpassing that level in some achievements but lagging behind in others.

Also, during the last period of their rule for some not fully understood reasons they where no longer contained to Americas but started to raid the rest of the world. The reason could be exploration or simple trade for the needed resources with barbarian tribes. And Atlantis finally achieved it by building superior ships which could cross Atlantic ocean. But as Plato says - they became corrupted and God punish them for corruption. So the more likely reason - raids to take slaves and resources from powerless tribes. It looks like Atlantis established some kind of puppet state or at least a port or station in Egypt, whose population considered them as Gods and where worshipping them during the latest period of their rules about 10,000 BC or even earlier. It is also clear, that Atlantes were original authors of ancient Antarctic maps drawing them during the period of global warming after the Great Ice Age ended - about 10,000 BC in summer and winter with more and less ice. And perhaps, Atlantis destroyed India using nuclear power about 9,800 - 9,900 BC because Indian Rama Empire (also know as Lemuria) begin its development around that time and maybe opposed or started posing a threat in the region for Atlantis. And because the Rama empire was so large and populous it was easier for Atlantis just to wipe it off the face of the Earth than rival with technologically inferior but huge and populous empire. The last statement is not so far fetched considering the definite fact that Atlantis had flying apparatus based on the multiple artifacts finding in Americas and Egypt. And, reviewing our own history we can learn that it took only 42 years for humanity from the first flight of an airplane lasting only 10 seconds performed by Wright Brothers in 1903 to a day long trans Pacific flight to drop a nuclear bomb on Hiroshima in 1945. Finally, according to Plato Atlantis met its own doom, by sinking into the ocean in a mighty cataclysm - not too long after the war with Rama Empire.

Previously described multiple artifacts and human remains dated before 12,000 BC (official date of populating America) confirm this theory. But skeptics still may not be satisfied and tell where are the major proofs like the excavated ancient cities in America? Here is at least one: Expedition of professor Polina Zelitsky, her husband Paul Vayntsvayg and their son Ernesto Tapancs found sunken stone megaliths and stone pyramid at a depth of 300 - 500 meters in the Caribbean sea near the peninsula Guanokohekabibe in south-eastern Cuba in 1990s. Megaliths covered with inscriptions in an unknown language with Egyptian resembling hieroglyphs. Another expedition in 2000s to same region - the western coast of Cuba, found flooded city of giant stones, megaliths, with the pyramids, plateau, rectangular buildings and roads. Samples were taken and tested to be from 6,000 to 12,000 years old.

Nano diamonds found in California.

Chapter 12: Lost Diamonds.

Now, let's find out what kind of cataclysm or what kind of earth shattering event spelled the doom for such a mighty civilization who inhibited at least two continents but ruled the whole world.

Nano-sized diamonds found embedded in the crust of Santa Rosa Island off the coast of Santa Barbara appear to have been formed when a comet crashed into Earth —the same comet that scientists say may also be responsible for the extinction of the island's pygmy mammoth. "The pygmy mammoth, the tiny island version of the North American mammoth, died off at this time," said UCSB professor emeritus James Kennett, who, with his son Douglas Kennett of the University of Oregon, led the 15-person research team whose findings were published this week in the Proceedings of the Natinal Academy of Science. "Since it coincides with this event, we suggest it is related."

Douglas Kennet said the hexagonal diamonds known as lonsdaleite are typically found in meteorites and impact craters; those in the sedimentary layer covering Santa Rosa Island known as Younger Dryas Boundary are evidence that a cataclysmic impact about 12,000 years ago scattered comet fragments across North America. James Kennet said that the diamonds' unique "assemblage of material" would not be possible without a long-ago cosmic blast.

The Santa Rosa diamonds were found under four meters of millenniums-old dust and soot telling a dark tale indeed. This layer was once airborne, the scientists hypothesize, sent skyward by the landing of the comet fragments—fragments that impacted with enough speed, heat, and force to produce not only dust, soot, and diamonds but extensive wildfires. Not enough sunlight could penetrate to enable the species survival. "This hypothesis fits with the abrupt climatic cooling as recorded in ocean-drilled sediments beneath the Santa Barbara Channel," Kennett said.

Thus, space rock slammed into the glaciers of eastern Canada about 12,000 years ago likely wiped out mega-animals like woolly mammoths and the continent first human inhabitants and very strangely coincide with the Plato's stated date of Atlantis doom or 9,700 BC.

This event was previously well know as the end of Great Ice age extinction event is characterized by the extinction of many large mammals weighing more than 40 kg (90 pounds). In North America about 35 of 45 genera of large mammals became extinct, in South America 47 of 58, in Australia 15 of 16, in Europe 9 of 23, and in Subsaharan Africa only 2 of 44. The extinctions in the Americas entailed the elimination of all the larger (over 100 kg) mammalian mega faunal species of South American origin, including those that had migrated north in the Great American Interchange. Only in America and Australia the extinction occur at family taxonomic levels or higher.

Have you ever wondered why there are almost no large animals in Australia, North and South America unlike in Africa and Eurasia? Now you know the answer: about 80% of all medium mammals genera and almost 100% of large mammals genera were killed (and large bears, wolves, bison and moose migrated later from Siberia). That event spelled doom not only for Atlantis but for wooly mammoths around the world. As a result of the extinction, there are very few large mammals are now found in Australia as well. Many types of large birds disappeared at that time too.

The theory says that an air burst and earth impact with a rare swarm of carbonaceous chondrites or comets set vast areas of the North American continent on fire, causing the extinction of most of the large animals in Americas and the demise of many large species at end of the last glacial period - about 10,000 BC. This swarm exploded above or into the Ice Sheet north of the Great Lakes. An airburst was similar to but many orders of magnitude larger than Tunguska event in Siberia in 1908. Animals and humans not directly killed by the blast or the resulting coast to coast wildfires would have starved on the burned surface of the continent.

Parts of the same comet, also know as Clovis comet most likely landed into Pacific and Atlantic oceans creating mega tsunamis described by almost all early civilizations as great flood. Any human structures around Great lakes area would have been obliterated to the dust and, therefore, they will never be found. Any Atlantis ports would also have been swallowed by giant tsunami. That's why archeologists found only scattered old remains of unexplained ancient cities: near Cuba, near Japan, near Canaries Islands, in Crimea Peninsula (Black Sea), in

Africa and America but never found a main core or a capital of that ancient civilization located somewhere at East Cost of North American continent and was completely annihilated by comet impact and earthquakes, tsunamis, fires and volcanic activity that follow. Even if Atlantis capital was not directly in the kill radius of the comet - it could be forever buried under volcanic lava and ashes caused by the comet or reduced to dust by an earthquake with magnitude over 10 on Richter scale created by the impact or washed away by the mega tsunami that follow, as Plato tells us, and forever gone from the face of the Earth. The effect is similar to sketching Roman Empire but never finding Rome or finding Babylonians but missing Babylon - the whole history of the world would have been written differently then.

Ancient Dinosaur from Central America.

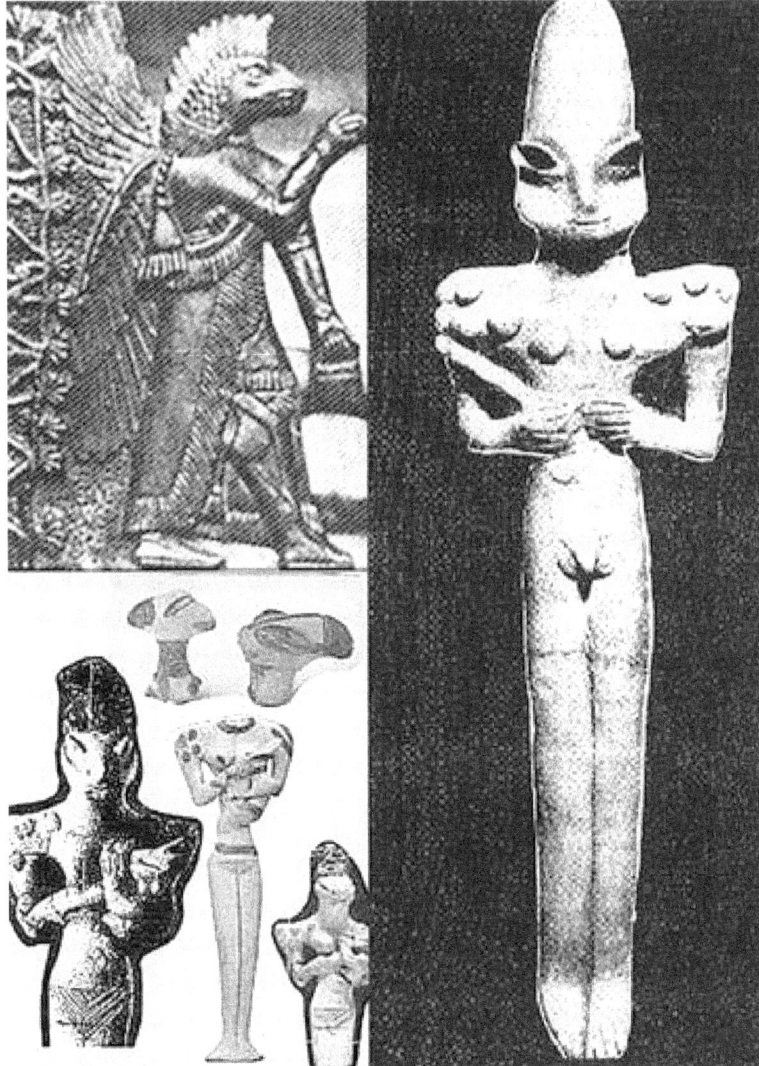
Very strange ancient figures from around the world.

Chapter 13: Exodus.

Certainly, not all Atlantes died out because of that comic disaster 12,000 years ago. By 9,700 BC they had cities, ports and stations around the world. Millions of people were populating once isolated empire 12,000 years ago. They all were not wiped out by that comet. Although, almost all Atlantes died in Americas at the day of the impact or shortly after because of burns and starvation the small group of people survived there and they are known to history as Clovis people. Officially, the Clovis culture is thought to have lasted for a very short period of time between 100 and 600 years, depending on the source consulted, with an average estimate of around 300 years only, starting about 12,000 years ago. Surprisingly, the Clovis short lived but complex culture was dissimilated and replaced by several more localized regional and more primitive cultures. A little doubt, that short lived Clovis culture was a degraded and primitive extension of post apocalyptic Atlantis in the same conditions the modern humanity would be after all-out nuclear war or a major asteroid impact.

However, there is one more time gap remains: from about 10,000 BC (destruction of Atlantis) to 3,000 BC (appearance of the first well known ancient civilization). Now we know that Clovis people, who populated North America right after the ancient disaster, were numbered only few thousands strong and very soon also died off or dissimilated into tribes arriving from Siberia. So the question remains: where the other Atlantis ancestors hiding for almost 7,000 years and why they finally decided to reveal themselves by staring known civilizations around 3,000 BC.

The devastation cased by Clovis comet and losing Americas meant the same for Atlantis like losing Italy and all surrounding islands for Roman Empire. It is clear, that most of the Atlantis technology and infrastructure were lost 12,000 years ago, but the remnants of once mighty civilization survived in the couple of outposts not washed by tsunamis or engulfed by earthquakes. There are several considerable candidates for such outpost cities outside devastated Americas. They are mentioned before: North Africa (where later mysteries artifacts were discovered), Crimea on Black Sea (where 37 mysterious pyramid build before Egyptians currently being unearthed), other places near North Africa - like Azores and Canary Islands, where unnatural landscape patterns were discovered using satellites and sonographs as well as many other Mediterranean Islands. Those surviving outpost could stretch as far as Cuba, North Sea and India where other unexplained later evidences were found. Of course, most of the mentioned places has not revealed a strong evidences belonging to a superior race yet but at least two or three o of them could yield clues to relate them to the remnants of the mighty but vanished Atlantic empire. It looks like that during the mentioned 7,000 years only a few such places survived and they remained more or less isolated from the surrounding world.

Around 3000 BC series of powerful volcanic eruptions occurred in Northern Africa and near North African and South European costal areas, some of them triggering huge tsunami which would dwarf 2005 Indonesian disaster. At least five large eruptions are recognized and recorded by geologists now: two in Azores, two in Northern Africa and one in Mediterranean. At the same time around 3000 BC the Henbury crater in Australia, Kaali crater in Estonia, and Burckle Crater in Indian ocean apparently were produced by object or objects which broke up before the impact and bombarded the earth with deadly chunks of asteroid - small and huge. The biggest of them newly discovered Burckle crater, 20 miles (33 km) in diameter, lies 12,500 feet (3,800 m) below the surface. This group posits that a large asteroid or comet impact 5,000 years ago, produced a mega-tsunami at least 650 feet (200 m) high. If this and other recent impacts prove to be correct, the rate of asteroid impacts is much higher than currently thought.

This fact also got conformation for an unlikely source - Assyrian cuneiform tablets written VIII century BC, kept in the British Museum, which was finally deciphered using computer program. Scientists struggled over its decryption the past 150 years. Now Brits Mark and Alan Bond Hempsell sure that artifact is a copy of notes Sumerian astronomer, made in the end of IV millennium BC (5,000 years ago or so). Watching the night sky, the ancient astrologer saw the asteroid and described it as "approaching white stone ball." Records indicate that the asteroid hit the Earth near the town of Kofels (unknown now town?). As a result, the territory of one million square kilometers was destroyed and all living things died in that area. Hempsell believed that disaster is reflected in at least 20 ancient myths, including the Old Testament story of Sodom and Gomorrah. "God destroyed them for their sinful depravity, sending a rain of sulfur and fire."

One of those catastrophic event spelled the final doom for remnants of Atlantes and forced them to flee their retreat city or cities and turn to nomadic tribes of Egypt and Mesopotamia and a little later to Southern Europe and Asia, and finally to South and Central America, transferring remains of their knowledge, religion and culture, explaining the mentioned earlier shocking similarities existing in different parts of world. Intelligent newcomers possessed knowledge and metal weapons never seen by primitive hunters and gatherers (who were using only stone and wood for their needs), therefore, they were regarded as deities, kings, and pharaohs of the ancient world. Their knowledge was transferred to their children, but it is obvious that newcomers did not arrive in large numbers and they could not build new Atlantis again and finally declined within a few centuries. But they intervention started the most significant event in ancient history: birth of several powerful civilizations we know today and their evolution leading to our modern society.

Ancient electric power battery found in Turkey.

Chapter 14: Troy.

Some skeptics could still argue that Atlantis is a myth and all mentioned artifacts and sites were left by other civilizations. However, the possible existence of genuine city of Troy was actively discussed throughout classical antiquity, but it was usually rejected and occasionally parodied by later authors. As one archeologist told to Heinrich Schliemann (who found Troy): "It is only in modern times that people have taken the Helen of Troy story seriously; no one did so in antiquity. It is nothing more than Homer lyrics and legendary love story."

However, Heinrich Schliemann (1822-1890), was determined to find the fabled city. It also may come as a shock to you but Schliemann never actually found Homer's Troy and "Priam's treasure" discovered by Schliemann never belonged to the king for which it was named. It was a remnant of a much earlier culture. He did find the site only. The Troy that he discovered was later called Troy I, dates from almost 3000 BC, the Early Bronze Age. Its ruins include brick walls and crude pottery. After Schliemann realized he had excavated too deeply, he found the treasure in the next layer up, now called Troy II, a city of stone walls with artifacts of finely worked metal. But this was still 1,000 years before the events of the Homer's *Iliad*.

After Schliemann's death in 1890, his widow vowed that his work would continue. She funded further excavations by Wilhelm Dörpfeld (1853-1940), who was more scientific in his orientation. He found nine separate cities, one on top the other, at the Troy site. He believed that the sixth of these was the Troy of the *Iliad*. It was larger than its predecessors, with high limestone walls protecting its perimeter, but never actually produced any stuffiest evidence and some skeptics still believed that the excavated city is just one of the Greek cities and had nothing to with "the love story" described in Homer's *Iliad*.

In 1932, a University of Cincinnati expedition led by Carl Blegen (1887-1971) studied the site. Like Dörpfeld, Blegen found nine layers, but recognized that Troy VI had been destroyed by an earthquake. This meant it wasn't Priam's city, fallen in a war or raid.

The city now proven to be the Troy of legend is the next layer, Troy VIIA. It is built of similar materials, as if rebuilt after the earthquake. But it lasted only about 100 years before being destroyed by fire and looting - Troy war.

Troy VIII, which stood while Homer actually lived, was a small Greek village. Troy IX was the city of Ilium, ruled by the Greeks and later by the Romans. Alexander the Great held athletic games there in the 300s BC to honor Achilles, from whom he believed himself to be descended. The city lasted until the reign of the Roman Emperor Constantine the Great in the 300s AD.

As you can see, some ancient cities like Troy contain ten layers left by different time epoch and, perhaps, by different civilizations placed on top of each other and it is very easy to scratch top or bottom layer only and say there is nothing of special interest buried there. It took almost 100 years to sort out all layers of Troy to find the exact layer the Homer was talking about. It is clear that many ancient cities, excavation sites and even some modern cities have even dipper secrets hidden beneath them. And if we, instead of placing unknown artifacts into the storages, start to investigate them and dig dipper layer by layer - like it was done in Troy - then we will reveal missing clues left by Atlantes civilization. For example, who knows what may be buried in the ground between levels VI and IX beneath your city?

Strange picture from ancient Minoan temple.

Chapter 15: Minoan.

Someone could ask: "Why bother? What is the difference - Atlantes in 13,000 BC or Egyptians in 3,000 BC? Why study so ancient history anyway?" First of all, discovered facts maybe holding keys to our own survival. It appears the rate of large asteroid and comets impacts to Earth is much higher than currently thought. For the last 12,000 years we can trace at least three major impacts that wiped out at least one civilization: 10,000 BC - Clovis comet that destroyed Atlantis and killed 80% of land mammal species in Americas and Australia; 3,000 BC - asteroids that punched 20 miles crater in Indian Ocean and produced mega tsunami; 1908 AD - Tunguska event in Siberia - over 1,000 times as powerful as the atomic bomb dropped on Hiroshima, Japan. Thus, for the last 12,000 years Earth survived at least 3 major cosmic bodies impacts. It won't be that hard to guess that the average time between impacts like this is about 5,000 years but not 200 million years like we learned in school. But cosmic bodies do not work like a clockwork and the next big impact could be well placed in our own or our children or grandchildren lifetime.

Second, people who forget history repeat it again because history has a tendency repeating itself and usually not in very pleasant forms.

Thus, not monoliths of ancient cities but a single olive branch may have solved one of ancient history's most enduring mysteries: "When and why did the great Minoan civilisation of the Mediterranean come to a sudden end?

The branch was buried during a cataclysmic volcanic eruption on the Aegean island of Thera - now known as Santorini - and scientists believe they can date the precise moment of the tree's death.

Knowing when the Thera eruption happened is important because the explosion was so powerful that it almost certainly caused the collapse of the Minoan civilization, centered on the island of Crete, 60 miles away. Vulcanologists believe the explosion generated violent tsunamis that destroyed Crete's ports, threw thousands of tons of ash and pumice into the atmosphere and created a "nuclear winter" that led to successive crop failures.

Scientists have detected ash from the explosion as far away as Greenland, the Black Sea and Egypt. They have also discovered signs of frost damage caused by the volcano on preserved plant material excavated in Ireland and California. Walter Friedrich, of the University of Aarhus in Denmark, and his colleagues have analyzed the olive branch's growth rings and combined the findings with radiocarbon dating to show the tree must have died between 1627 BC and 1600 BC.

"It is important to have a very precise date for the explosion because this eruption is a global time marker. If we can date it precisely we have an important tool to correlate the times of different cultures," Dr Friedrich said.

Tom Pfeiffer, a student of Dr Friedrich, discovered the olive branch buried inside a rock face formed from volcanic debris. The researchers are convinced the tree was alive when it was smothered. The scientists found 72 growth rings, including the final year ring, inside the branch. Using radiocarbon dating, they worked out the year of the tree's death to an accuracy of 13 years each way.

The study, published in the journal Science, suggests Thera blew apart a century or so prior to the conventional date when the Minoan civilization was thought to have gone into demise, based on evidence from archaeological objects. The scientists suggest it is highly unlikely the Minoans were able to survive the environmental impact of the eruption, which meant their civilization ended 100 to 150 years earlier than thought. This would mean the Minoan civilization was not contemporary with the New Kingdom of ancient Egypt - which began in the 16th century BC - as many archaeologists believed.

A separate study published in Science by Professor Sturt Manning of Cornell University in New York shows radiocarbon dating of 127 objects recovered from the Theran town of Akrotiri - which was buried by the eruption - support the findings."

Professor Colin Renfrew, a Cambridge archaeologist, said the studies appeared to provide convincing evidence to put a firm date on the eruption in Thera.

History, indeed, did repeat itself: first by annihilating Atlantis in Americas and then using the other natural cataclysm to get rid from the other powerful and advanced - Minoan civilization in Mediterranean.

Ancient Babylonian Tree of Life.

Another Ancient Flying Creature Found in Mexico.

Chapter 16: Evolution.

Does not this early powerful civilization scenario in direct contraction to Darwin Theory of evolution? Let's see: The Mammal-like Reptiles, or Therapsids first appeared almost 300 millions years ago - near the beginning of the Permian which is well before the dinosaurs. They evolved quickly and many different groups arose. They were very successful until about the end of the Permian, about 245 million years ago, when something catastrophic affected the earth and nearly all of the species then living died out. New species evolved rapidly to fill this empty habitat, among them the first dinosaurs and a few million years later the first mammals.

The first mammal may never be known, but the Genus *Morganucodon* and in particular *Morganucodon watsoni*, a 2-3 cm (1 - 1.5 inch) long weasel-like animal whose fossils were first found in caves in Wales and around Bristol (UK), but later unearthed in China, India, North America, South Africa and Western Europe is also a possible contender. It is believed to have lived between 200 and 225 millions years ago.

The evolution conventional theory says that it took about two millions years from the first monkey using the first tool evolve to the first human doing a moonwalk. Based on Pluto writings and scientific findings we assume that Atlantes or their successors existed in a period somewhere between several hundreds thousands years ago and 9,700 BC. It is scientifically proven (using DNA tests, anatomically, physiologically, genetics research, computer simulated environmental modification research, etc) that two or thee millions years is enough for ape to evolve into a human, it is also scientifically proven that 70 million years is more than enough for several hundred pounds giant dinosaur to evolve into light weight colorful bird. So where is the contraction in theory of evolution saying that it took not 210 million of years for motioned above 1 inch weasel-like animal in evolve into an intelligent human like ape but only 209 millions years?

What about the earlier evidences? Like mentioned 30 millions years old artifacts? Are they all improperly dated or fakes? Could be, however, lets review another more fantastic scenario that could also be true, unless proven otherwise.

Hundreds years from now a huge spacecraft with antimatter engine and dozens of astronauts lands at an distant planet in other solar system with planetary condition similar to ours (presence of water, breathable atmosphere, stable surface, etc) to investigate alien life. Because of their very long trip and events described in my previous book Future History (2006) they no longer interest earthlings and virtually loose all communication and have no means necessary to return back to Earth. What those future astronauts-expeditors world do? Logically, establish a colony around their space ship. They would be very lucky if the planet is indeed inhabited. If it is a case, they would use some species directly for meal and conveniences, and cultivate and genetically modify others to fit their needs. Technology would allow them to enhance most advanced species and give them some brainpower to service their needs. Technology would also allow them to live for hundreds if not thousands years. Technology which astronauts brought with them would be very reliable but still it could not last for thousand years. They will be the true gods of this alien earth-like planet but eventually they will pass away, but before doing so passing they knowledge to their children. Who probably would need to build more primitive power plants from whatever materials available to keep remains of earth tech to function. But eventually, their children will die too passing whatever is left to grandchildren. There is only one foreseeable outcome: degradation. Degradation of former earthlings but the unimaginably huge leap for primitive creatures populating the planet who where genetically enhanced and bestowed with huge amount of knowledge by newcomers.

Why would still existing and seemingly well-being Earth humanity would loose interest in space exploration and not to send the rescue mission or any other missions to such interesting Earth-like planet? It is almost impossible to belive now that in a few hundreds of years when "holy grail" of all modern hopes and dreams of contact with alien live is at fingertips, Earth turns its back to it. Yes, why? Please, read my previous book Future History: Complete history of the future from 2006 AD to 100 billion AD - about quarter of this book is dedicated to answering these questions.

Now imagine the same scenario, with an alien spaceship visiting earth 20 million years ago. Cut off, they desperately trying to survive. They found plenty of resources on Earth but they don't have means to explore them. Their robots or bio-robots have limited power supply and, therefore, life span. Even if their technology is high enough to allow self replication of those alien servants (which is unlikely) - their number is still very limited and not nearly enough to mine needed resources to built a power plant to power their spacecraft and techs they bought.

At the same time Earth already had plenty of monkey species and, possibly, the first apes beginning to evolve. Those visitors most likely did not have time to make selective breeding live early humans breed horses, dogs, pigs, cows, etc to fit our needs. Instead, like modern humans they used methods of genetic enhancement and modification like modern day creation of allergy free cats in 2009, genetically health improved pigs in 2008, and transgenic goats who supply human proteins for some drugs making since 2009 as well. Buy the way, you can buy a tropical fish genetically modified to glow in the dark that went on sale for about $17 each since 2003 at any major local fish and pet store. Or a different variety of zebrafish, called "GloFish," which was genetically enhanced to glow in the dark too since 2005 for about $5 each. So if nowadays cost of genetic modification or improvement is only $5, you can only imagine what civilization capable of interstellar traveling is able to do. Most likely, it would add some brainpower and enhance desirable features to prehistoric apes and employ them at primitive jobs such as mining, serving, simple constructions, etc.

Should it be the true story - it would be a good answer to scientists who claim that human brain is the most complex known thing in the universe that several millions of years not is not enough to develop it form banana pilling to computer programming. But as long as no one unearthed that first alien spaceship that claim would remain just a fascinating fantastic theory.

From other hand, back to the aluminum copper platinum plated alloy shown me at UC Berkley. It is resembles modern substance alloy called 2024-T used in applications requiring high strength to weight ratio, as well as good fatigue resistance such as space industry and 5th generation jet fighter planes. But it also has to poor corrosion resistance, so it is often clad with Zink for protection, although this may reduce the fatigue strength. So perhaps, aliens or their successors had abundance or Platinum which does not reduce the straight but very expensive. Such alloy was invented in 1970s with Zink and still did not exist and no records of production with Platinum as better Zink substitute. Remember that the piece of this metal alloy was found in late 1840s - 10 years before Aluminum was first produced in its pure form and 130 years before 2024-T was invented. In the middle of nineteen century this most abundant metal on Earth cost many times than gold because aluminum was exceedingly difficult to extract from its various ores. Thus, bar of Aluminum was the most precious item in jewelry collection of French imperator Napoleon III. Aluminum also was selected as the material to be used for the apex of the Washington Monument in 1884 - its price have fallen but it still cost more than silver. No wonder, American Indians were worshipping to this precious alloy as if it indeed come to them from God's boat.

Ancient Astronaut or Aqualungs Sculpture.

Natural rock formations in Turkey.

Chapter 17: Human Place in History.

65 million years ago. Asteroid or comet impact or solar minimum or whatever cataclysm caused dinosaurs to extinct did not happen. Dinosaurs ruled land and sea for over 100 millions years and without that dramatic impact they would continue to do so for the next 65 million years. Certainly, they would evolve into more sophisticated species and predatory birds, which would wipe out the remaining mammals, leaving only a few most adopted and smallest mostly underground mammal species to live, which does not include vulnerable and weak monkeys - a perfect prey for hungry dinosaurs and gigantic predatory birds. It is proven that some survived dinosaurs evolved into huge non flying birds, which were preying on mammals such as first horses and primitive monkeys. Imagine the world where you have to be sized less than a mice and live underground to be unseen by a hungry carnivorous bird on an ugly predatory reptile. That would be the modern world if the cosmic disaster missed us 65 million years ago.

600 thousand years ago. The Great Ice Age did not start because of the constant solar activity. Only 12,000 years ago over 1/3 of the planet surface was ice and snow. Because of the Ice Age arrival, primitive humans had to invent

tools, lean to keep fire, fry foods, boil water, wear clothes, build houses, create more advanced hunting and survival techniques, invent animal traps, stone knifes and spears in order to survive. And then, perhaps, about 25,000 years ago they evolved into superior society which give roots to most of other known ancient civilizations. Anyway, had The Coolest Ice (650,000 - 600,000 BC) and The Great Ice Age (40,000 - 10,000 BC) never occurred, primitive humans would continue enjoy plenty of warm weather and food abundance. Thus, human evolution would slow down and modern mankind would probably get busy not by planning a manned mission to Mars but by trying to make a better spears to hunt or a more convenient baskets to gather berries and a bow and arrow would be an invention of the millennium.

45 years ago. Caribbean Crisis led to the full scale nuclear war. Billions would die because of the nuclear strikes and the war side effects such as world wide radioactive fallouts and nuclear winter. Forty years later Earth population would be totaling less than a billion of people dramatically struggling for their survival in the conditions similar to middle ages, desperately trying to rebuild planet infrastructure to the level it was in 1960s.

Now is year 2009 and it appears that we humans cast in iron and set in stone our rightful place in history not only in a couple of continents, not even on entire Earth but in the whole Solar system. Let's review this statement more closely. Yes, humans are undoubtedly the most dominant species the Earth has ever known. In just a few thousand years humans have swallowed up more than a third of the planet's land for our cities and farmlands. And we are leaving quite a mess behind: ploughed-up prairies, razed forests, drained aquifers, nuclear waste, chemical pollution, invasive species, mass extinctions, etc. The other species we share Earth with would surely vote us off the planet if they could.

Now just suppose the other species got their wish. Imagine that exaggerated prophecy of doom of 2012 turns out to be correct and all the people on Earth - almost 7 billions vanish or perish December 21st of 2012.

"Left once more to its own devices, Nature would begin to reclaim the planet, as fields and pastures reverted to prairies and forest, the air and water cleansed themselves of pollutants, and roads and cities crumbled back to dust. The sad truth is, once the humans get out of the picture, the outlook starts to get a lot better," says John Orrock, a conservation biologist at the National Center for Ecological Analysis and Synthesis in Santa Barbara, California. But would the footprint of humanity ever fade away completely, or have we so altered the Earth that even a million years from now a visitor would know that an industrial society once ruled the planet?

If tomorrow dawns without humans, even from orbit the change will be evident almost immediately, as the blaze of artificial light that brightens the night begins to fade out. Indeed, there are few better ways to grasp just how utterly we dominate the surface of the Earth than to look at the distribution of artificial illumination. By some estimates, 85 per cent of the night sky above the European

Union is light-polluted; in the US it is 62 per cent and in Japan 98.5 per cent. In some countries, including Germany, Austria, Belgium and the Netherlands, there is no longer any night sky untainted by light pollution.

"Pretty quickly - 24, maybe 48 hours - you'd start to see blackouts because of the lack of fuel added to power stations," says Gordon Masterton, president of the UK's Institution of Civil Engineers in London. Renewable sources such as wind turbines and solar will keep a few automatic lights burning, but lack of maintenance of the distribution grid will scuttle these in weeks or months. The loss of electricity will also quickly silence water pumps, sewage treatment plants and all the other machinery of modern society.

The same lack of maintenance will spell an early demise for buildings, roads, bridges and other structures. Though modern buildings are typically engineered to last 60 years, bridges 120 years and dams 250, these life spans assume someone will keep them clean, fix minor leaks and correct problems with foundations. Without people to do these seemingly minor chores, things go downhill quickly.

The best illustration of this is the city of Pripyat near Chernobyl in Ukraine, which was abandoned after the nuclear disaster 20 years ago and remains deserted. "From a distance, you would still believe that Pripyat is a living city, but the buildings are slowly decaying," says Ronald Chesser, an environmental biologist at Texas Tech University in Lubbock who has worked extensively in the exclusion zone around Chernobyl. "The most pervasive thing you see are plants whose root systems get into the concrete and behind the bricks and into doorframes and so forth, and are rapidly breaking up the structure. You wouldn't think, as you walk around your house every day, that we have a big impact on keeping that from happening, but clearly we do. It's really sobering to see how the plant community invades every nook and cranny of a city."

With no one to make repairs, every storm, flood and frosty night gnaws away at abandoned buildings, and within a few decades roofs will begin to fall in and buildings collapse. This has already begun to happen in Pripyat. Wood-framed houses and other smaller structures, which are built to laxer standards, will be the first to go. Next down may be the glassy, soaring structures that tend to win acclaim these days. "The elegant suspension bridges, the lightweight forms, these are the kinds of structures that would be more vulnerable," says Masterton. "There's less reserve of strength built into the design, unlike solid masonry buildings and those using arches and vaults."

Even though buildings will crumble, their ruins - especially those made of stone or concrete - are likely to last thousands of years. "We still have records of civilizations that are 3,000 years old," notes Masterton. "For many thousands of years there would still be some signs of the civilizations that we created. It's going to take a long time for a concrete road to disappear. It might be severely crumbling in many places, but it'll take a long time to become invisible."

The lack of maintenance will have especially dramatic effects at the 430 or so nuclear power plants now operating worldwide. Nuclear waste already consigned to long-term storage in air-cooled metal and concrete casks should be fine, since the containers are designed to survive thousands of years of neglect, by which time their radioactivity - mostly in the form of cesium-137 and strontium-90 - will have dropped a thousandfold, says Rodney Ewing, a geologist at the University of Michigan who specializes in radioactive waste management. Active reactors will not fare so well. As cooling water evaporates or leaks away, reactor cores are likely to catch fire or melt down, releasing large amounts of radiation. The effects of such releases, however, may be less dire than most people suppose.

The area around Chernobyl has revealed just how fast nature can bounce back. "I really expected to see a nuclear desert there," says Chesser. "I was quite surprised. When you enter into the exclusion zone, it's a very thriving ecosystem."

The first few years after people evacuated the zone, rats and house mice flourished, and packs of feral dogs roamed the area despite efforts to exterminate them. But the heyday of these vermin proved to be short-lived, and already the native fauna has begun to take over. Wild boar are 10 to 15 times as common within the Chernobyl exclusion zone as outside it, and big predators are making a spectacular comeback. "I've never seen a wolf in the Ukraine outside the exclusion zone. I've seen many of them inside," says Chesser.

The same should be true for most other ecosystems once people disappear, though recovery rates will vary. Warmer, moister regions, where ecosystem processes tend to run more quickly in any case, will bounce back more quickly than cooler, more arid ones. Not surprisingly, areas still rich in native species will recover faster than more severely altered systems. In the boreal forests of northern Alberta, Canada, for example, human impact mostly consists of access roads, pipelines, another narrow strips cut through the forest. In the absence of human activity, the forest will close over 80 per cent of these within 50 years, and all but 5 per cent within 200, according to simulations by Brad Stelfox, an independent land-use ecologist based in Bragg Creek, Alberta.

In contrast, places where native forests have been replaced by plantations of a single tree species may take several generations of trees - several centuries - to work their way back to a natural state. The vast expanses of rice, wheat and maize that cover the world's grain belts may also take quite some time to revert to mostly native species.

At the extreme, some ecosystems may never return to the way they were before humans interfered, because they have become locked into a new "stable state" that resists returning to the original. In Hawaii, for example, introduced grasses now generate frequent wildfires that would prevent native forests from re-establishing themselves even if given free rein, says David Wilcove, a conservation biologist at Princeton University.

Feral descendants of domestic animals and plants, too, are likely to become permanent additions in many ecosystems, just as wild horses and feral pigs already have in some places. Highly domesticated species such as cattle, dogs and wheat, the products of centuries of artificial selection and inbreeding, will probably evolve back towards hardier, less specialized forms through random breeding. "If man disappears tomorrow, do you expect to see herds of poodles roaming the plains?" asks Chesser. Almost certainly not - but hardy mongrels will probably do just fine. Even cattle and other livestock, bred for meat or milk rather than hardiness, are likely to persist, though in much fewer numbers than today.

What about genetically modified crops? In August, Jay Reichman and colleagues at the US Environmental Protection Agency's labs in Corvallis, Oregon, reported that a GM version of a perennial called creeping bentgrass had established itself in the wild after escaping from an experimental plot in Oregon. Like most GM crops, however, the bentgrass is engineered to be resistant to a pesticide, which comes at a metabolic cost to the organism, so in the absence of spraying it will be at a disadvantage and will probably die out too.

Nor will our absence mean a reprieve for every species teetering on the brink of extinction. Biologists estimate that habitat loss is pivotal in about 85 percent of cases where US species become endangered, so most such species will benefit once habitats begin to rebound. However, species in the direst straits may have already passed some critical threshold below which they lack the genetic diversity or the ecological critical mass they need to recover. These "dead species walking" - cheetahs and California condors, for example - are likely to slip away regardless.

Other causes of species becoming endangered may be harder to reverse than habitat loss. For example, about half of all endangered species are in trouble at least partly because of predation or competition from invasive introduced species. Some of these introduced species - house sparrows, for example, which are native to Eurasia but now dominate many cities in North America - will dwindle away once the gardens and bird feeders of suburban civilization vanish. Others though, such as rabbits in Australia and cheat grass in the American west, do not need human help and will likely be around for the long haul and continue to edge out imperiled native species.

Ironically, a few endangered species - those charismatic enough to have attracted serious help from conservationists - will actually fare worse with people no longer around to protect them. Kirtland's warbler - one of the rarest birds in North America, once down to just a few hundred birds - suffers not only because of habitat loss near its Great Lakes breeding grounds but also thanks to brown-headed cowbirds, which lay their eggs in the warblers' nests and trick them into raising cowbird chicks instead of their own. Thanks to an aggressive program to trap cowbirds, warbler numbers have rebounded, but once people disappear, the warblers could be in trouble, says Wilcove.
On the whole, though, a humanless Earth will likely be a safer place for threatened biodiversity. "I would expect the number of species that benefit to significantly exceed the number that suffer, at least globally," Wilcove says.

In the oceans, too, fish populations will gradually recover from drastic over fishing. The last time fishing more or less stopped - during the second world war, when few fishing vessels ventured far from port - cod populations in the North Sea skyrocketed. Today, however, populations of cod and other economically important fish have slumped much further than they did in the 1930s, and recovery may take significantly longer than five or so years.

The problem is that there are now so few cod and other large predatory fish that they can no longer keep populations of smaller fish such as gurnards in check. Instead, the smaller fish turn the tables and out compete or eat tiny juvenile cod, thus keeping their erstwhile predators in check. The problem will only get worse in the first few years after fishing ceases, as populations of smaller, faster-breeding fish flourish like weeds in an abandoned field. Eventually, though, in the absence of fishing, enough large predators will reach maturity to restore the normal balance. Such a transition might take anywhere from a few years to a few decades, says Daniel Pauly, a fisheries biologist at the University of British Columbia in Vancouver.

With trawlers no longer churning up nutrients from the ocean floor, near-shore ecosystems will return to a relatively nutrient-poor state. This will be most apparent as a drop in the frequency of harmful algal blooms such as the red tides that often plague coastal areas today. Meanwhile, the tall, graceful corals and other bottom-dwelling organisms on deep-water reefs will gradually begin to re-grow, restoring complex three-dimensional structure to ocean-floor habitats that are now largely flattened, featureless wastelands.

Long before any of this, however - in fact, the instant human vanish from the Earth - pollutants will cease spewing from automobile tailpipes and the smokestacks and waste outlets of our factories. What happens next will depend on the chemistry of each particular pollutant. A few, such as oxides of nitrogen and sulphur and ozone (the ground-level pollutant, not the protective layer high in the stratosphere), will wash out of the atmosphere in a matter of a few weeks. Others, such as chlorofluorocarbons, dioxins and the pesticide DDT, take longer to break down. Some will last a few decades.

The excess nitrates and phosphates that can turn lakes and rivers into algae-choked soups will also clear away within a few decades, at least for surface waters. A little excess nitrate may persist for much longer within groundwater, where it is less subject to microbial conversion into atmospheric nitrogen. "Groundwater is the long-term memory in the system," says Kenneth Potter, a hydrologist at the University of Wisconsin at Madison.

Carbon dioxide, the biggest worry in today's world because of its leading role in global warming, will have a more complex fate. Most of the CO_2 emitted from burning fossil fuels is eventually absorbed into the ocean. This happens relatively quickly for surface waters - just a few decades - but the ocean depths will take about a thousand years to soak up their full share. Even when that equilibrium has been reached, though, about 15 per cent of the CO_2 from burning fossil fuels will remain in the atmosphere, leaving its concentration at about 300 parts per million compared with pre-industrial levels of 280 ppm. "There will be CO_2 left in the atmosphere, continuing to influence the climate, more than 1000 years after humans stop emitting it," says Susan Solomon, an atmospheric chemist with the US National Oceanic and Atmospheric Administration (NOAA) in Boulder, Colorado. Eventually calcium ions released from sea-bottom sediments will allow the sea to mop up the remaining excess over the next 20,000 years or so.

Even if CO_2 emissions stop tomorrow, though, global warming will continue for another century, boosting average temperatures by a further few tenths of a degree. Atmospheric scientists call this "committed warming", and it happens because the oceans take so long to warm up compared with the atmosphere. In essence, the oceans are acting as a giant air conditioner, keeping the atmosphere cooler than it would otherwise be for the present level of CO_2. Most policy-makers fail to take this committed warming into account, says Gerald Meehl, a climate modeler at the National Center for Atmospheric Research, also in Boulder. "They think if it gets bad enough we'll just put the brakes on, but we can't just stop and expect everything to be OK, because we're already committed to this warming."

That extra warming we have already ordered lends some uncertainty to the fate of another important greenhouse gas, methane, which produces about 20 per cent of our current global warming. Methane's chemical lifetime in the atmosphere is only about 10 years, so its concentration could rapidly return to pre-industrial levels if emissions cease. The wild card, though, is that there are massive reserves of methane in the form of methane hydrates on the sea floor and frozen into permafrost. Further temperature rises may destabilize these reserves and dump much of the methane into the atmosphere. "We may stop emitting methane ourselves, but we may already have triggered climate change to the point where methane may be released through other processes that we have no control over," says Pieter Tans, an atmospheric scientist at NOAA in Boulder.

No one knows how close the Earth is to that threshold. "We don't notice it yet in our global measurement network, but there is local evidence that there is some destabilization going on of permafrost soils, and methane is being released," says Tans. Solomon, on the other hand, sees little evidence that a sharp global threshold is near.

All things considered, it will only take a few tens of thousands of years at most before almost every trace of our present dominance has vanished completely. Alien visitors coming to Earth 100,000 years hence will find no obvious signs that an advanced civilization ever lived here.

Yet if the aliens had good enough scientific tools they could still find a few hints of our presence. For a start, the fossil record would show a mass extinction centered on the present day, including the sudden disappearance of large mammals across North America at the end of the last ice age. A little digging might also turn up intriguing signs of a long-lost intelligent civilization, such as dense concentrations of skeletons of a large bipedal ape, clearly deliberately buried, some with gold teeth or grave goods such as jewelry.

And if the visitors chanced across one of today's landfills, they might still find fragments of glass and plastic - and maybe even paper - to bear witness to our presence. "I would virtually guarantee that there would be some," says William Rathje, an archaeologist at Stanford University in California who has excavated many landfills. "The preservation of things is really pretty amazing. We think of artifacts as being so impermanent, but in certain cases things are going to last a long time."

Ocean sediment cores will show a brief period during which massive amounts of heavy metals such as mercury were deposited, a relic of our fleeting industrial society. The same sediment band will also show a concentration of radioactive isotopes left by reactor meltdowns after our disappearance. The atmosphere will bear traces of a few gases that don't occur in nature, especially perfluorocarbons such as CF_4, which have a half-life of tens of thousands of years. Finally a brief, century-long pulse of radio waves will forever radiate out across the galaxy and beyond, proof - for anything that cares and is able to listen - that we once had something to say and a way to say it.

But these will be flimsy souvenirs, almost pathetic reminders of a civilization that once thought itself the pinnacle of achievement. Within a few hundred thousand years, erosion and possibly another ice age or two will have obliterated most of even these faint traces. If another intelligent species ever evolves on the Earth - and that is by no means certain, given how long life flourished before we came along - it may well have no inkling that we were ever here save for a few peculiar fossils and ossified relics. The humbling - and perversely comforting - reality is that the Earth will forget us remarkably quickly."

Now, imagine, not that incomprehensibly distant future - year 400,000 AD. Alien spacecraft landed on deserted earth and aliens found a variety of wild living species. All earth structures even such as mighty river dams and concrete bunkers are reduced to dust and no any detectable leftovers of Earth circling satellites left. They surveyed the whole planet for possible signs of current and previous intelligence and found only a few land and marine mammals possessing very primitive intelligence signs. Some parts of strange skeletons with large skulls suggesting presence of intelligence are unearthed but after further studies concluded - they belong to an extinct breed of two legged monkeys and possess no further interest. However, a group of alien astronauts unearth a very few strange glass and metal objects and found a weird mountain with rock formations resembling alien faces which they claimed to be the products of past intelligence life. Later studies by conducted by reputable alien archeologists concluded that all metal and glass objects are created during asteroid impacts and volcanic activity and strange mountain is just a weird natural rock formation. Thus, mountain

Rushmore shared its fate with the Face of Mars hills and all humanity traits are discarded and forever forgotten.

Ancient 3D hologram of gold nail in Amber.

Famous Ancient Mayan Calendar.

Epilogue: Mayan Calendar.

What about the artifact considered by many to be the greatest of all: Mayan super calendar saying that world will end 12.21.2012? Let's dismiss the tons of incompetent prophecies that world will end in 2012 as many unreasonably believe. This year (2012) may mean the birth of the new better world but by no means our generation is the last one to inhabit the planet. For some supernatural reasons almost every generation believed that they are the last people to see the Sun because the Judgment Day, Armageddon or Last Judgment will occur and Christ or Antichrist will ensure the imminent end in just a few years or, at least, the Earth will stop rotating or turn upside-down and all things on its surface will fall right into the hell. According to these "prophesies" if that's won't happen then Moon and Sun will fall on Earth for sure. Almost every turn of century was proclaimed as the last one, almost every significant event was treated as an imminent sign of the nearing doom. The new popular theories: overdue killer asteroid impact, Earth poles flip, or super volcano wiping all planetary life by dispersing tons of hot ashes and evaporating the oceans are rather amusing than to be considered real within the next few centuries. I am personally simply fascinated by the "ingenious" idea of a tiny invisible black hole swallowing the whole solar system in an blink of an eye vividly which was described in details by a group of "prominent" scientists a couple of years ago. The true end of times will indeed happen in the very distant future and well described in my previous book Future History: Complete history of the future from 2006 AD to 100 billion AD.

Indeed, Mayan civilizing inherited some high-tech features from previously described advanced predecessor civilization. But scholars are bristling at attempts to link the ancient Maya with trends in contemporary spirituality. Maya civilization, known for advanced writing, mathematics and astronomy, flourished for centuries in Mesoamerica, especially between 300 and 900 AD. Its Long Count calendar, which was discontinued under Spanish colonization, tracks more than 5,000 years, then resets at year zero.

"For the ancient Maya, it was a huge celebration to make it to the end of a whole cycle," says Sandra Noble, executive director of the Foundation for the Advancement of Mesoamerican Studies in Crystal River, Fla. To render Dec. 21, 2012, as a doomsday or moment of cosmic shifting, she says, is "a complete fabrication and a chance for a lot of people to cash in."

Part of the 2012 mystique stems from the stars. On the winter solstice in 2012, the sun will be aligned with the center of the Milky Way for the first time in about 26,000 years. This means that "whatever energy typically streams to Earth from the center of the Milky Way will indeed be disrupted on 12/21/12 at 11:11 p.m. Universal Time," Joseph writes. How does ancient Maya figured it out? Well, they did not but were given this knowledge by advanced predecessor civilization, you can call them Atlantis if you like because all astronomers generally agree that "it would be impossible the Maya themselves would have known that," says Susan Milbrath, a Maya archaeo-astronomer and a curator at the Florida Museum of Natural History. What's more, she says, "we have no record or knowledge that they would think the world would come to an end at that point."

University of Florida anthropologist Susan Gillespie says the 2012 phenomenon comes "from media and from other people making use of the Maya past to fulfill agendas that are really their own." Indeed, many spiritual institutions such as churches, cults and commercial instructions such as crisis battled store chains and companies as well as self proclaimed authors, prophets, media companies and even some politicians are exploiting 2012 doomsday perdition like they did decade ago exploiting 2YK millennium scare to full their pockets with money. All new millennium scare is created for one single purpose: to earn money and has little to do with ancient Mayans or even with their predecessors Atlantis.

However, this scare is indeed turns out to be so big that it affects everyone's mind and clear way of judgment leading to a new mass hysteria. And, mark my words, at best, some crazed sect will commit mass murder-suicide in 2012 or 2013 the latest, or at worst, a group of calculating terrorists will detonate a nuclear or biochemical device around the doomsday date but it will have a little to do with Milky Way galaxy alignment.

Ancient Sumerian Science.

Appendix I: Approximate Ancient Timeline.

7,000,000 BC. Orrorin and Sahelanthropus appear.

5,000,000 BC. Orrorin and Sahelanthropus migrate to Americas and Australia.

4,000,000 BC. Australopithecus and Ameropithecus evolve.

3,000,000 BC. Humans use primitive tools.

2,000,000 BC. Humans use fire.

1,000,000 BC. Humans spread around the world.

650,000 BC. The coldest Ice Age on Earth.

600,000 BC. Humans make clothes, shoes, built houses.

35,000 BC. The Great Ice Age begins.

30,000 BC. First known civilization Atlantis appear in Americas.

15,000 BC. Atlantes cross Atlantic ocean.

14,000 BC. Atlantes cross Pacific ocean.

13,000 BC. Atlantis establish trade, resources, slave roots around the world.

12,000 BC. Atlantis establish outposts in Egypt and few other places.

11,000 BC. Rama civilization or Lemuians appear in India.

10,000 BC. Golden Age of Atlantis.

9,900 BC. Atlantis destroys Rama empire.

9,800 BC. Clovis comet destroys Atlantis civilization.

9,700 BC. Survivors known as Clovis people in America.

9,600 BC. Couple of Atlantis outposts survived impact and tsunamis and rebuilt.
.
9,500 BC. Clovis people in America face starvation, die out and dissimilate.

3,300 BC. Volcanic activity starts in North Africa and surrounding islands.

3,200 BC. Burckle asteroid creates mega tsunami.

3,100 BC. Remnants of Atlantis dissimilate to the world.

3,000 BC. Egyptian civilization appear.

2,900 BC. Sumerian civilization appear.

2,800 BC. Minoan civilization appear.

2,600 BC. Indus civilization appear.

2,500 BC. Akkad civilization appear.

2,400 BC. Chinese civilization appear.

2,300 BC. Mayan civilization appear.

2,200 BC. Babylonian civilization appear.

2,100 BC. Assyrian civilization appear.

2,000 BC. Hittite civilization appear.

Appendix II: About the Author.

Igor Kryan was born in 1979 in Kiev, Ukraine. He arrived to the Unites States in 1999 and happily married in 2004 in San Francisco, California. The author graduated with Honors in National Ukrainian Medical University (AA Degree in Health Science - 1999), San Francisco State University (BS degree in Biology - 2003), New York Vernell University (Master of Fine Arts - 2003), Amsterdam Ravenhurst University, Netherlands, (MS degree in Cell and Molecular Science - 2004). He is also a bearer of many awards in art and science.

Igor Kryan started his writing career in 2003 by publishing a short brochure of historical essays called "Answers." But the author was already known for his graphic art works and the brochure come unnoticed by the public and only 100 copies were ever printed. However, in 2005 Igor Kryan decided to modify his astrobiology research performed for Amsterdam Ravenhurst University, and published another book called "The Source." This book had an overwhelming success - thousands copies were sold and many more are being currently sold across the globe. The pervious book "Future History: Complete history of the future from 2006 AD to 100 billion AD" this 100 page book incorporated "The Source" and was published in 2006 and it was the most complex, challenging and daring work the author have ever created. The current book "History of The Impossible: Earth before the Pyramids" No one before had ever attempted to design a systematic and chronological work of the major unknown ancient events with scientific and historical explanations. The true history of the past was finally revealed by one man.

www.ingramcontent.com/pod-product-compliance
Lightning Source LLC
LaVergne TN
LVHW081336060426
835513LV00014B/1318